SURVIVING MENTAL ILLNESS

My Story

LINDA NAOMI KATZ

outskirtspress

DENVER, COLORADO

Surviving Mental Illness
My Story
All Rights Reserved.
Copyright © 2012 Linda Naomi Katz
v3.0 r1.0

Outskirts Press, Inc.
http://www.outskirtspress.com

ISBN: 978-1-4327-8399-0

Library of Congress Control Number: 2012901589

Outskirts Press and the "OP" logo are trademarks belonging to Outskirts Press, Inc.

PRINTED IN THE UNITED STATES OF AMERICA

In Dedication

To the Memory

Of My Beloved

Parents

David and Helga

Baron

ABOUT THE AUTHOR

Linda Naomi Katz was born on March 21, 1969, raised in the Jewish faith by both parents who sent her to a Modern Orthodox Day School. Mental illness became a factor in her family when she was in the fifth grade. Her mother suffered from a breakdown and developed depression which became difficult for the entire family. As Linda was growing up towards adulthood, her mother's illness affected her too and was depressed most of the time which became difficult for her to make friends, develop positive relationships, or get a job. At the age of 24, she also developed mental illness and was diagnosed with bipolar disorder. Being a modern orthodox woman, Linda soon discovered how biased and stigmatized the orthodox community was towards her having a mental illness. It became very hard, especially when she was trying to develop serious relationships. However, with her belief in God and Judaism, she never stopped trying to fight her way back towards recovery. Today she is happily married, has a Bachelor of Arts degree from the City University of New York at Queens College, and continues her work as a mental health advocate.

TABLE OF CONTENTS

CHAPTER ONE

WHAT IS MENTAL ILLNESS?

When most people think about the mentally ill, they assume that such people are insane or crazy, or perhaps even freaks. However, that is not true. Mental illness is a disease of the human mind, which can disrupt a person's thinking, feeling, mood, ability to relate to others, daily functioning at work, school, or in activities they once liked. Mental illness also makes it difficult for someone to distinguish between the real and the unreal world. In the real world, people who suffer from mental illness cannot avoid the pain or the pleasure in their life. In the unreal world, these people try to hide their pain and create fantasies or images which they would very much like to be real.

Mental illness is caused by a combination of factors such as heredity, biological reasons, psychological trauma, and environmental elements. With heredity, sometimes mental illness runs in families, passed on from parents to children through their genes. Biologically, some mental illnesses are tied to a chemical imbalance in the brain. These chemicals are known as neurotransmitters and affect thoughts, emotional, and behavioral responses, which may cause changes in making rational judgments, moods (being too happy or too sad), and how one functions in everyday life. Some mental illnesses come from psychological trauma suffered as a child, such as emotional or physical abuse, loss of a parent, or neglect. Environmental stresses, such as a death or divorce, changing jobs or schools, or substance abuse issues, can trigger a disorder in a person who may be at risk for developing a mental illness.

In today's society, most people still put a stigma on those who have a mental illness. What is a stigma? Stigma is a negative judgment or severe disapproval of a person based on characteristics that distinguish them from other people in society. People who do not have a mental illness and do not understand it, can sometimes make bad judgments and think that the mentally ill are not normal. The truth is that people with mental illnesses are normal like everyone else and can lead productive lives, if they are given the chance.

Why is there such stigma against those with a mental illness? What do people have to fear? Simply, they fear the unknown. Most people are not educated enough about mental illness because they do not want to understand it, while others do not want to have anything to do with the mentally ill for selfish reasons. This kind of thinking is nothing but a shame in today's times. The more that people are educated and able to change their way of thinking about mental illness, the better life can be for people with mental illness and those around them.

There are many types of mental illnesses, but the ones that I want to focus on are mood disorders. The three major types of mood disorders are major depression, bipolar disorder, and schizophrenia. Before anyone can seek treatment, one has to admit that they have a problem, and that can be difficult to do. Some fear that they will never be able to work because an employer might not hire them. Others fear that they will never get married if their mental illness is discovered. These fears result from stigma all over the world. However, if the condition is not treated, some will always be unemployed, be homeless, possibly be incarcerated, or commit suicide.

Today, mental illness is treatable with medication and therapy. There are agencies which assist in recovery by helping individuals find a job, go back to work, establish a support group where they can meet friends, or even date other people who also have a mental illness. These agencies help people realize they are not alone.

In this chapter, I will discuss the three major types of mood disorders and discuss the treatments that are available. I will also go in depth as to how recovery from mental illness is possible and can be achieved.

The most common type of mental illness is major depression. It is a serious medical illness that affects fifteen million Americans or about five to eight percent of the adult population in a given year. It is brought on by a combination of symptoms that can interfere with a person's ability to work, study, and sleep. Some of these symptoms include persistent sadness, uncontrollable crying, difficulty concentrating or making decisions, feelings of guilt and worthlessness, loss of appetite, loss of interest, and pleasure in hobbies or activities once enjoyed.

Major depression can also cause people to commit suicide which is one of the leading causes of death in the United States. Suicide does not have to happen if people can admit to themselves that they have a problem and seek treatment immediately. Even when they are in treatment, suicide can occur, but the risk is much lower for those who do seek treatment. For example, the loss of a loved one, the loss of a job or home, being incarcerated, or engaging in drug abuse, can all trigger suicide. Suicide victims feel so down with life that they lose hope because no one takes the time to reach out to them. If these victims seek support from agencies that can help them find homes, employment, learn how to cope with life by being around loved ones, and stay on their medications, they can start a better life.

Major depression can be treated by a psychiatrist and/or a therapist. A psychiatrist prescribes medications and a therapist discusses major life problems that result from having the condition. Some medications the psychiatrist will prescribe for depression are Celexa, Paxil, Wellbutrin, and Prozac. These may have some side effects, such as headaches, nausea, dry mouth, and dizziness. These side effects should not make a person stop taking the medication, because doing so could be dangerous. A person could fall into a relapse and experience more symptoms of depression, becoming worse than before.

Having a therapist to talk to about whatever problems someone is facing may help them deal with the depression and also help the way they interact with people, by going from negative to positive behavior. This is why it is so important to have a combination of medication and therapy. Without the two, it can be difficult to treat any type of mental illness.

The second type of mood disorder is known as bipolar or manic depression, which is what I suffer from. I have already described what depression is as well as its symptoms. Mania is a condition in which one's mood changes from a normal state to an overactive state. Mania often affects your rational thinking, judgment, and social behavior. This can cause serious problems and embarrassment. In the manic phase, one may feel elated and euphoric, a state described as being "on top of the world." Some symptoms of mania include restlessness, a decreased need for sleep, talking rapidly, having racing thoughts, experiencing grandiose notions, and increased energy. Sometimes, the manic state progresses to the point where judgment is impaired and contact with reality is lost. This can cause poorly thought out decisions acted on impulsively, such as calling a friend in the middle of the night or going on a shopping spree. A person can also have psychotic symptoms like hallucinations or delusions, such as hearing voices or believing one has special powers. Bipolar disorder can go from extreme highs to low depressed moods. This extreme mood swing can be triggered by psychological, environmental, and genetic factors that I discussed earlier in this chapter.

There are different medications that are used in treating bipolar disorder. The most common medication psychiatrists recommend is Lithium. Lithium can stop a manic episode from occurring and prevent further manic depressive episodes from coming back. However, this medication has to be carefully monitored and is not for everyone (especially if one has a thyroid or kidney problem). The other major medicines that treat bipolar disorder are known as anticonvulsants, such as Tegretol, Depakote, and Lamictal. These medicines can help stabilize one's mood and, just like Lithium, can stop further episodes from occurring again. Medicines that can control certain psychotic symptoms during a manic depression like hallucinations are known as antipsychotics. Schizophrenics also use antipsychotics to treat their symptoms.

With bipolar disorder, medications may not be enough. Just as in major depression, getting therapy and attending support groups may help relieve some problems in a person's life and help understand why these symptoms appear. Therefore, it is very important to seek help.

The third major mood disorder, which affects one percent of Americans, is schizophrenia. This is a serious brain disorder that distorts the way a person thinks, acts, perceives reality, and relates to others. People with schizophrenia often have problems functioning in society, at work, at school, and in relationships. Schizophrenia is a psychosis, a type of mental illness in which a person cannot tell what is real from what is imagined. As I explained earlier with bipolar disorder, individuals can develop psychotic symptoms as well. This can be confusing and some people can be misdiagnosed. However, with an illness like schizophrenia, it is so much more than hearing voices or believing in things that are not real. For instance, people may not make sense when they talk, and may have difficulty holding a job or caring for themselves.

Although treatments are available, schizophrenia will remain with sufferers all their lives, and some symptoms may never go away. For example, some people may repeat certain motions over and over again, and in extreme cases, some may be catatonic. This occurs when individuals are in a state of immobility and cannot respond to a simple question. As with bipolar disorder, those with schizophrenia have difficulty making decisions because their thoughts are not organized. Schizophrenics can also suffer from depression. They often feel isolated from the rest of the world and cannot find pleasure in everyday life. Schizophrenia may be hard to overcome because of the symptoms I described to you.

There are three main types of schizophrenia. These types are paranoia, disorganization, and catatonia. Individuals who are inflicted with paranoid schizophrenia have delusions or false beliefs about being persecuted or being punished by someone. Disorganized schizophrenia occurs when people are confused, incoherent, and have jumbled speech. Their behavior is silly or childlike, and they may have trouble doing the simplest things like showering and preparing meals. Those with catatonic schizophrenia are unable to respond to the world around them. As a result, schizophrenia is a major mood disorder which is the most difficult to overcome.

However, schizophrenia *can* be treated with medication and therapy. Most psychiatrists recommend antipsychotics to alleviate some symptoms of the disease. Some antipsychotics are *Risperdal*, *Abilify*, *Zyprexa*, *Prolixin*, *Haldol*, and *Seroquel*. The length of treatment can be life long, since schizophrenia needs constant management. If a person does not get treated, relapses can occur even when the person feels better. Therapy is important too. A therapist can help patients understand and adjust to living with schizophrenia by educating them about its causes and the symptoms they may experience. Therapists also help schizophrenics communicate better and care for themselves.

With all of these mental illnesses that I described to you, recovery is possible. A psychiatrist and therapist can inform patients about organizations that will assist them in getting a job, making new friends, dating people, improving their hygiene, or in getting housing and entitlements.

One such organization is called *NAMI*. It stands for the National Alliance of the Mentally Ill. *NAMI* is an agency that provides support, education, and advocacy for families and individuals who live with mental illness. This agency encourages families to share their struggles and talk about their symptoms and treatments through support groups. Some support groups for individuals with mental illness offer concern for diagnoses of major depression, bipolar disorder, and schizophrenia. For example, *New York City Voices*, a journal for the mentally ill that works with *NAMI*, offers a group called *Awakenings*. This group is only for individuals who want to talk about their diagnoses, its treatments, and how to relate to people in today's society. Other groups offer support for parents who have trouble relating to a child that has a mental illness. The *NAMI* chapter in New York City has a support group called, "*Family and Friends of Individuals with Mood Disorders*." This group helps parents to understand their child's mood disorder and how it affects them.

NAMI also keeps the community informed by sending out newsletters about its programs and services as well as the latest news in treatment medications, public policy, and legislation. This helps in the fight against stigma. Earlier in this chapter, I spoke about what it is like to be faced with stigma. People who have negative views on mental illness assume that the mentally ill are dangerous. These people do not even want to try to understand that mental illness is a disease that can be treated through medications and therapy. *NAMI* deals with stigma by reaching out to the community through media, such as the internet, radio, television, newspapers, ads, and magazines. *NAMI* also informs the community on how to become a "*Stigma Buster*" for the mentally ill. *NAMI StigmaBusters* is a network of dedicated advocates across the country and around the world who seek to fight inaccurate and hurtful representations of mental illness.

StigmaBusters' goal is to break down the barriers of ignorance, prejudice, or unfair discrimination by promoting education, understanding, and respect. *NAMI* sets up people who have mental illness with others who also have mental illness. *NAMI* helps them socialize by taking them on trips, picnics, and movies. For example, the *NAMI* branch in Queens/Nassau has organized, *"The Friendship Network."* This organization provides a service in which they match a person with someone else who has a similar background. If a person is Jewish, they will be set up with someone who is also Jewish, and thus share their same values, faith, and beliefs. The *Friendship Network* also plans a variety of activities for their members such as tennis, bowling, workshops for nutrition, trips to museums, and movies. As you can see, *NAMI* does a tremendous amount of work to educate the public about mental illness.

For those individuals with mental illness who want to recover by going back to work, employment programs are available to help a person get a job whether it's full-time, part-time, an internship, or a volunteer position. Some of these programs include clubhouses, supported employment, and pre-vocational. Clubhouses are programs that offer its members a place to belong. This allows them to develop relationships with other individuals and to gain meaningful work. Clubhouses believe that work is essential for recovery from mental illness. Members can volunteer their time in a clerical unit, an employment unit, and a food service unit. This helps individuals gain experience and prepare for the business world. Clubhouses also offer transitional employment which provides its members with part-time positions lasting six to nine months. This gives them a chance to gain work experience outside the clubhouse. In addition, they help members get their own jobs within the community by providing various levels of support.

Supported employment programs help individuals with mental illness to gain real jobs that are competitive in today's job market. Each of these jobs is based on a person's abilities and career goals. Individuals are offered support on or off the job site in order to retain their jobs. Some supported employment programs are sponsored by *VESID*, the Office of Vocational and Educational Services for Individuals with Disabilities. *VESID* recognizes that all persons with disabilities can benefit from vocational rehabilitation services and should have opportunities to work within their community. In these programs, counselors guide individuals through the transition from school to work, job training and placement, and other services to support their employment goals.

On the other hand, pre-vocational programs focus mainly on preparing these individuals to enter the workplace. For example, *PROS*, Personalized Recovery Oriented Services, is designed to help these individuals think about and select goals related to employment, housing, education, wellness, socialization, and writing. Pre-vocational programs are helpful to persons with a mental illness who do not have much work experience and need help focusing on a career path. They offer a variety of activities to help these persons identify their interests and skills, learn about work alternatives, and help them develop a plan for selecting and obtaining work.

Almost all of these programs, (clubhouses, supported employment, and pre-vocational) teach individuals with mental illness how to write a resume, job seeking skills, how to act in a job interview, and how to dress for success.

Based on what I have written in this chapter, one can now understand the three types of mood disorders and how to focus on recovery through some agencies that I have mentioned.

In the next few chapters, I will discuss how mental illness had a big impact on my family and me. I hope that by discussing my struggles with mental illness, you will understand how a mentally ill person can overcome fears and focus on recovery from a disease that will be with them for the rest of their life.

CHAPTER TWO
MY FAMILY'S HISTORY OF MENTAL ILLNESS

Mental illness has been in my family's genes since my grandfather's time. I believe that when my grandfather was imprisoned in Germany in the 1930's during World War II, it may have caused him to develop a mental illness early in life. At the prison, he was tortured and took a lot of abuse from other prisoners. When a person is tortured, their mind also becomes afflicted. They fall into a depressive state and act differently in the way they interact with people. In my grandfather's days, I don't think anyone knew what mental illness was, and therefore he lived for years without seeking treatment.

When I was a year old, my grandfather suffered a stroke and was never again the same mentally. He became very stubborn and would not seek any help from a physician. He often blamed my father for the stroke he had, was stingy when it came to money, and persuaded my mother not to earn a living. After the stroke, my grandfather just wanted to die. He lost his perspective in life and would refuse to go anywhere, and instead, just stayed in bed. My grandfather also started to act like a dictator and tried to control his wife (my grandmother). For instance, if he wanted to sleep, she had to sleep. If he wanted to eat, she had to eat too. Since he could not travel, my grandmother was also unable to travel and this made life for her unbearable. She could not even leave the house unless she told him where she was going. My father could not get along with him either. Once, my father got so upset that he refused to go to my grandparents' home anymore. Years later, my grandfather's mental illness would have an affect on my mother.

My mother was a loving, caring person and when she married my father, she was so happy. She was very strong and I looked up to her. I remember visiting her at work once, thinking that one day I would work in an office like she did. My mother helped the family whenever she could. When I was in the second grade, she made pilgrim costumes for the play that my class was in. She also helped my father with his work because she was very artistic. These were nice memories that I had of my mother, but these times would not last long.

When my father was out of a job and my mother was working, her father (my grandfather) used to play mind tricks on her when he called her at work. He often told her that she should quit her job and that her husband should be the breadwinner. This was a way for my grandfather to control her mind. Between her father, my father, and taking care of me, my mother snapped and suffered a nervous breakdown. I was confused and did not understand what was happening to my mother. I remember how scared I was of her, and looking at her face with fear, as if there were huge bumps on her forehead. When my mother had the nervous breakdown, my father picked me up from school early and we took her to the doctor.

Shortly thereafter, my parents went to their primary care

physician who told them that my mother was mentally ill, and he sent her to a psychiatrist at a hospital in Hempstead, Long Island. From that point on, my father had to be the one to take charge. He not only had to be a father, but a mother as well. My father was in a lot of pain and suffered so much from my mother's mental illness that taking care of us became too much of a burden for him. I was always amazed at how he remained strong.

During this time, my mother stayed in a psychiatric ward of a hospital for two to three weeks while her psychiatrist tried to stabilize her mood through a variety of medications, until one worked. He finally found two medications that worked for her. They were *Prolixin* and *Symmetral*. *Prolixin* is an antipsychotic used to stop certain symptoms like hearing voices, racing thoughts, and poor judgment. *Symmetral* was used to control the side effects of the *Prolixin* medication. Although I was told by my father that her doctor diagnosed her with having acute depression, I think she had bipolar disorder or schizophrenia. The symptoms she had and the medications that were prescribed for her, make me now think that she had a different mood disorder.

My mother said things that she really did not mean, but it was not her fault. The mental illness she had took control of her mind. Not only did she hear voices and had racing thoughts, but she believed that my father was her enemy. My mother was also confused about her religion as a Jew. She had thoughts that convinced her to become an orthodox Jew. These thoughts told her to go to a *mikvah* (a ritual bath to regain purity) and purify herself, even though my mother was a conservative Jew. She often fought with my father and tried to force him to be orthodox. This made sense to me in a way because I was attending an orthodox yeshiva (Jewish day school). Although my father tried to be patient, he lost his cool and started to fight back. I suffered emotionally and cried every time I heard them fight.

My mother's psychiatrist recommended to my parents that they seek therapy to discuss their problems. However, my mother would not hear of it. Life at home did not get any better for us as a family. My parents had terrible fights about my mother taking her medications. Sometimes she would throw away her pills in the toilet, and other times forget to take them. When my mother took her pills, she was like her normal self. However, we could not trust her. My father and I had to take turns at night and bring pills to her to be sure that she would take them. This situation lasted for several years.

My mother also wanted to divorce my father who cared for her deeply. After her illness, the love that they had for each other was not the same. Her psychiatrist did not think their marriage would last. When my parents spoke of divorce, I became very depressed. I never liked the thought of divorce and told my father that my mother did not know what she was talking about and that she needed him whether she realized it or not. Eventually, my father decided to make the sacrifice and keep the family together.

When my father decided not to divorce my mother, he did it for two reasons. One reason was that he knew my mother could not make it on her own because she was not good at making decisions, and with her mental illness, he realized she would be a lot worse than she was at that time. The second reason was because of me. I was still very young and still in school and needed both my parents.

My father finally concluded that a divorce would tear the family apart and I feared that I would never see my mother again if this were to happen.

After my mother's illness, my parents' social life was not good. It was hard for my mother to make friends. Sometimes she would say things that were not rational and did not make sense. It was difficult to take her anywhere. The friends she had either ran away from her or kept their distance. Because my father had many friends and relatives, he could not take her out to any gatherings. There were times she said stupid things she did not mean and had trouble understanding the Arabic language that my father's family spoke. As a result, my mother began to feel more isolated and alone.

My father also felt alone. He was afraid to make any new friends and feared how my mother would react towards them. Even when my father was the educational director of the synagogue we belonged to, he felt embarrassed watching my mother serve food to the members who played Bingo. He thought my mother should have a more prestigious job because of his position at the synagogue. All of this was due to her mental illness which did not allow her to socialize very much, and for which I think she should not have been blamed for.

I did not understand everything about her mental illness and did not know how much of it would have an impact on me later in life. I did not want to become like my mother, but even when I was young, I feared that I would develop a mental illness just like hers.

CHAPTER THREE
THE BEGINNING

Although I was not diagnosed with having a mental illness at a younger age, the illness may have started during my teenage years. It probably developed through the struggles we had with my mother's illness.

When I went to public school in Baldwin, Long Island, I did not have many friends and always felt isolated and alone. At the time, my father worked for a few companies in the field of accounting but always dreamt of going back to work as a principal for afternoon Hebrew schools. When I was 14 or 15 years old, my father got a job in New Jersey and decided it was time for the family to move away from Baldwin and make a fresh start because there were too many bad memories as a result of my mother's mental illness. I did not want to move. I liked Baldwin, even though I did not have many friends there. As far as I was concerned, it was the only place I knew growing up as a child.

The stress of even thinking about moving caused me to have pains in my stomach. I was in so much discomfort that I went to see a gastrologist who could not find anything wrong with me. One day the pain was so bad, that I was rushed to the hospital. The doctors and nurses ran some tests and finally discovered that I had kidney stones. However, the doctor told my parents that the pain in my stomach was probably due to a psychosomatic illness.

I missed two weeks of school and it was hard for me to catch up. One of my teachers let me take an open book exam. She told me not to tell any of the students in the classroom that I was given special consideration because I was sick. When she finished grading the exams, I accidentally told some students that my test was an open book exam. The teacher looked at me and I felt guilty about it, so I wrote her a letter telling her how sorry I was and that I would never do this again. She gave the letter to my guidance counselor who knew I was showing signs of depression. He called my parents and told them that I needed to see a psychiatrist. My father spoke to my mother's psychiatrist and he recommended I see a psychologist in Plainview, Long Island. My psychologist was friendly, and we talked about what I did in school and how moving from Baldwin had affected me. At that time, my father was supposed to begin his new job which was to start in the summer in Fair Lawn, New Jersey. The psychologist recommended that I see another psychologist by the name of Dr. Arnold Sperling in Fair Lawn, New Jersey, once I got settled in school and had adjusted to the move.

I started seeing Dr. Sperling at the start of the school year. I talked to him about my problems of adjusting to a new place and how making friends was difficult for me. He showed me some biofeedback techniques to relieve the stress I was experiencing. The biofeedback techniques were very effective in treating me because they taught me how to relax. I remember the machines he used on me and it felt like the whispering tones to a song. This process, he explained, was called meditation. Dr. Sperling also helped me understand that making friends takes some time, especially when you are living in a new neighborhood and going to a new school. I stayed with him for a whole year. Afterwards, I did not need to use his services anymore because I became adjusted to where I was living and had made lots of friendships that developed over the year. As a result, I felt that he had accomplished his task with me.

When I became a junior, I decided to see the social worker in my school instead of Dr. Sperling, because I had gotten better. The social worker was very nice. I saw her often and talked to her about my difficulties in school, at home, etc.

Before the start of my senior year, I had problems deciding what courses to take that would be helpful for a career in business after graduation from high school. I was beginning to show signs of depression again, and cried to my guidance counselor and parents because I was unsure as to what to do with my life. The guidance counselor told me that I did not have to make any decisions until after college. I was relieved. I was glad that I was not taking courses in computers and decided to take a course in accounting instead, since part of me wanted to major in business.

Throughout high school, I knew I was not a happy teenager. I always knew I had some symptoms of depression because I used to cry frequently every time someone got angry with me for doing something wrong. During my senior year, I felt anxious and nervous about my plans for the future such as going to college and how difficult it would be to start over in a new environment. This is why I always saw the social worker at my school because I knew deep down there was something wrong with me. Even though my depression was not serious enough to diagnose as a mental illness, it was the beginning of it.

After graduating from high school, my parents put the house up for sale because my father's position at the synagogue was terminated. It also made sense to move again since I had been accepted to Queens College. My family found an apartment in Forest Hills, Queens, and we moved there the start of the school year. I was shifting to a new school and environment. My parents were still struggling with the house in Fair Lawn, since it was not yet sold. This move caused my family and me a lot of stress. Moving to a new place and meeting new people were difficult adjustments for all of us, but this time I was excited and not depressed, since I was starting to develop a new life for myself. This new life affected me in ways that would change my personality and growth into adulthood.

When I started going to Queens College, I decided to check out the Jewish life on campus. In the Student Union, there were many clubs to get involved with, but what interested me was *B'nai Brith Hillel/Jacy*. The day that *Hillel* had an open house, I met a girl who told me to come to a board meeting. Before the start of the meeting, there was this boy who I was attracted to and wanted to get to know. He showed up at this meeting and was involved in a club called *Kesher*. This was an Israeli club on campus that fought for Israel and was a part of the *Council of Jewish Organizations*. I knew from the start that the meeting in *Hillel* was not a place where I belonged to just yet, so I left. However, I could not stop thinking about this boy, and he became the start of my many troubles.

This boy stayed on my mind and I slowly developed a crush on him. I began to do everything I could to get to know about him, so a friend of mine introduced me to him. His name was Al. One day, I asked him to take me to a dance that *B'nai Brith Hillel* was sponsoring. When he picked me up, I did not expect to find other people with him, since I assumed this was a date. Realizing that it was not a date, I told my friend what happened and that I liked him. When Al heard that I had a crush on him, he was very flattered. We talked at the dance, and the more we talked, the more I grew to like him. However, he had a girlfriend who he introduced me to, so I decided to become his friend. After the dance was over he drove me home, but I could not shake the feelings I had for him. I did not know what these feelings were or what they meant, but I knew they were leading me into a dangerous infatuation.

In the meanwhile, I was glad to be his friend. The more our friendship grew, the more intense my feelings for him became. I did whatever I could to be close to Al, and found myself getting involved in *Kesher*. I also became somewhat friendly with his girlfriend. I felt safe when he was dating someone because it was a way to keep my feelings from him hidden. However, I did not realize the love that I had for Al was really an infatuation, and not something real. An infatuation is a foolish type of love for someone based on what your mind sees in that person. I had liked the qualities that Al had since they were very similar to my father's. Al had leadership and fought for everything he believed in. In this way, I felt he was like my father, and fell instantly in love with him.

When Al eventually broke up with his girlfriend, I did not handle it very well. I became emotional with him and could not keep my feelings for him hidden any longer, so I told him that I loved him. Al did not know what to say to that. Not only did I tell him that I loved him, I wrote letters to him. This was a big mistake, since Al did not feel the same way.

Two weeks later, Al told me not to call him, write to him, or talk to him anymore. I was very heartbroken, and for three weeks I stayed in a deep depression. I could not concentrate on my school work and felt so depressed that I did not want to go to school. Since Al and I shared the same friends, it felt very uncomfortable being around him. I could not believe that liking someone was like a crime, which added to my depression.

After three weeks, we started talking again as if nothing happened, but I knew that our friendship was not the same as it was before. As a result, I started seeing a counselor at the college who helped me through the pain of my depression and made me understand that my love for Al was not real.

I met with the counselor every two weeks and I continued to see her throughout my years at Queens College. I talked to her about other problems I had, such as choosing a major, and my family. Most of all, I talked to her about Al.

Even after Al graduated college, he still came around. Not only did I see him around campus, but also at my synagogue and at parties for singles within the New York City area. We managed to stay friends and still kept in touch by phone. I was happy about that, but still had hope that one day we would be together.

In my junior year of college, I went to study for a semester at *Tel Aviv University* in Israel. After the flight, I was anxious, tired, and emotionally upset because of the amount of waiting time it took to settle in and find my room which I would soon share with someone else. Later, my father came to Israel for a week. While he was there, the director of the *Overseas Student Program* told him how depressed I was and how she thought it would be in my best interest to leave the program. However, my father would not hear of it and convinced the director to let me stay as long as I saw a psychologist on campus. After my father left, things got easier. I studied and traveled all over the country. I saw some relatives and it was fun. Seeing the psychologist made me feel good about myself. She helped me become more independent and outgoing during my stay in Israel.

By the time Passover came, my father's relatives wanted me to spend the *seder* (a ritual dinner observed during Passover) with them, but instead I went to my mother's family in Jerusalem, since they were more religious. It was very different from the *seders* my father had. For some reason, I started to get homesick. I telephoned my parents and told them how depressed I was, so my father told me to go and see his family. That week was very difficult for me and I wished that I was home with my own family for Passover.

When classes started again, I felt much better and told the psychologist how homesick I had been during Passover. She tried to help me as best as she could, but the depression had already taken over my mind and body.

After this, my parents thought it would be a good idea for me to go to England after the program was over. They wanted me to explore England and tour places like Buckingham Palace and possibly visit some relatives. The more I thought about it, the more nervous I became. I was worried about where I would stay and how I would manage by myself, and I panicked. The director noticed that my depression was worse and made me call my parents and tell them that I did not want to go to England. My father calmed me down and said that I should not go in light of the situation, and that I should come home immediately after the program was over.

Despite my ups and downs while living in Israel, I was still happy that I got a chance to study and explore Israel on my own. Nonetheless, the depression that I had gone through made me think that one day I would have to seek help for it.

At the beginning of my senior year in college, my grandfather passed away. My mother received a phone call from her mother that her father was "ice cold." This meant my grandfather probably died during the night while sleeping. My father quickly drove me to school and then went to see my grandparents. When I came home, my father told me that our grandfather had died. The first person I worried about was my mother. When she came home, I saw how depressed and sad her face was. I was worried that she was going to have another nervous breakdown even though she was taking medication for her depression. My mother had every right to cry and be depressed, but as long as she continued treatment, I knew she was going to deal with his death in a mature manner. At the funeral, I saw my grandfather's body and cried but stayed strong for my mother's sake. Having to deal with a death in the family was hard and it affected me in a bad way because I was close to him. We were also worried about my grandmother living alone because she had trouble seeing and hearing. Eventually, my father helped her buy an apartment in the same building we lived in. It amazed me as to how my mother got through this because the loss of my grandfather affected us all. As a result, we dealt with his death as a family, which was enough support for all of us.

After I graduated college, I stopped seeing the counselor on campus and went to seek employment in the financial sector of New York City. I went on many tiresome job interviews. Six months after graduation, I was hired by an insurance company. After three days, I was fired because I was too slow. I ended up crying on the telephone to my father. A month later, I got a temporary position at *Republic National Bank* doing photocopying and filing. For the first few months, I was doing fine. Later on, I started making a lot of mistakes and wondered if the business world was for me. Working as a temp and going on job interviews made me anxious and exhausted. I became so depressed that I did not want to get out of bed, could not eat, and started to hate work. I decided to quit and became very depressed because I did not have a job. My father spoke to Dr. Jack Nass, my mother's psychiatrist, and scheduled an appointment for me to see him. Dr. Nass thought I could overcome the depression on my own, and that I did not need to take any medications at that time, since there are many people who get depressed because they do not have a job. However, he suggested that I seek therapy to overcome this problem.

In July 1992, I started seeing a therapist at the *Advanced Center for Psychotherapy*. It was an outpatient clinic where people with psychiatric disorders sought therapy. My therapist, Ruth Mutzner, was a very nice person who helped me with a lot of problems I was having

with my family, seeking employment, and in building relationships
with other people.

At this point in my life, I was not sure of what career to pursue.
I only knew that the business world was not the right environment
for me to be in. I decided to go back to school for a Masters in
Library Science. However, I was not sure about this field and whether I would find work in it. The director in charge of the *Masters in
Library Science* program noticed that I was in a deep depression and
suggested that I leave the program. I felt so alone and depressed that
I thought my whole universe and the way I perceived life was about
to end. Consequently, I decided to do some volunteer work at the
Forest Hills Community House. It was around this time that everything in my life came tumbling down and I knew that nothing was
going to be the same ever again. As a result of all of these things that
had happened, I suffered a nervous breakdown.

CHAPTER FOUR
HOW I WAS DIAGNOSED WITH BIPOLAR DISORDER

In 1993, I suffered a nervous breakdown which frightened me and my family. I had no idea what I was doing. I felt as if I was in another universe that was not real. I had trouble sleeping, had racing thoughts going through my head, heard voices, had grandiose notions, and talked rapidly. When my parents realized that I might have a mental illness like my mother had, my father called Dr. Nass and told him all about my symptoms. Shortly thereafter, Dr. Nass told us to come and see him. The doctor took one look at me and diagnosed me with manic depression/bipolar disorder.

As I stated in chapter one, manic depression/bipolar disorder is a radical change in a person's mood, where they alternate from being very depressed to being in an overactive state. I will describe some of the manic episodes that occurred during my nervous breakdown.

In 1993, I had my first manic attack. The first time this happened frightened my family, yet in my mind, I was on top of the world. It started with Al, the boy that I had an infatuation with during college. I could not get him out of my mind. I heard a variety of voices in my head, but none of them were as powerful as those

I heard about Al. I thought these voices were real, so I listened to them. I told my friends that Al was my boyfriend, when in reality he was not. When I volunteered at *Forest Hills Community House*, a senior citizen center, I met an elderly woman who I thought was Al's grandmother, and a young woman who I believed was his sister. Once, when the community house took the senior citizens to *Flushing Meadows Corona Park* to visit a museum, another racing thought about Al came to my mind. In this thought, I believed I was getting married to him and having his five children. When I told these things to my friend, she told me that Al did not have a sister and that I was not going to be married to him because he did not feel the same way. Can you imagine what my friends thought of me?

During that same time, I went to see the *Hillel* director at Queens College, and for some reason, told him that Al and I were getting married. I had no idea what was wrong with me. At *Hillel*, I went from room to room going crazy as I looked for him because I kept hearing him call my name. The director knew that I was not being myself and believed I was on drugs. He called my father and asked him to come right away. My father knew immediately that I was suffering from some type of mental illness, the same way my mother had. He told the *Hillel* director that I was not on drugs, but was mentally troubled.

At times, I would have hallucinations, as if I were viewing them on a TV screen. One hallucination was that Al and I got married and several of our friends from Queens College were our bridesmaids and ushers. Of course, this was not real, and after a few sessions with Dr. Nass, I began to see the light and realize the reality of my situation. This world I was in was so unreal that when the delusions started to fade away gradually, I began to wake up, as if coming out of a dream. I could not understand where these voices, thoughts and hallucinations were coming from. It is hard to understand how the mind works, but I knew that my mind would not let me do or say such things, unless there was a part inside me that wanted all this to be true.

Sometimes with bipolar disorder, one loses contact with reality. The mind begins reacting with poor judgment and one acts impulsively. Once, when I woke up at 6 a.m., I heard Al's voice inside my head telling me to call him at that hour. When I heard him answer the phone, I could tell he was very tired. He asked me not to call him anymore, so I hung up, but somehow I wondered why I was not hurt by his remarks. As soon as I woke up to this reality, I realized what I had done. I felt so guilty because I had lost control of my mind. I could not blame Al if he stayed angry at me forever. I also heard the voice of his mother telling me to call her too. When my father heard about it, he said, "This is wrong! The woman could take you to court!" I had no idea why I acted so impulsively, and if I did, I knew I was not to blame, since this was part of my manic phase.

Sometimes, when having bipolar disorder, one develops manic episodes, believing they are the Messiah or a highly special type of religious person. Religion and spirituality have always been a part of my life as a modern orthodox Jewish person. Once, I had a manic episode when I was lying on my sofa in the living room. I believed I heard the voices of people from *Queens College Hillel* praying to me outside my window as if I was the Messiah or some very special prophet. As I know now, this was not real, but very much felt like it.

While I was going through this phase, I started seeing Dr. Nass, my mother's psychiatrist. He put me on an antipsychotic medicine known as *Prolixin*, but kept encouraging me to take *Lithium*, a medication that could prevent further manic episodes from returning. I refused to take the medication because of the serious side effects *Lithium* had. I thought an antipsychotic like *Prolixin* would be enough to control the psychotic symptoms that came during my manic and depressive states, but this was not so.

After one year, another manic episode occurred. This time the mania led me to see a psychic to solve my problems and bring Al closer to me. I paid the psychic $2,500. When my father came back from Israel, I told him what had happened and he was furious. He knew that I was not in a healthy mental state, so he calmed down. The next day, my father went to the psychic with two police officers and forced her to return the money or go to jail. I had let a psychic take advantage of me and if I had been thinking clearly, this would never have happened.

After this, I started hearing Al's voices again. Once, I went into a bookstore and started talking to a strange man when I thought he was Al's father. I also went on shopping sprees. My parents asked me to go to Walgreens for a few items and I ended up buying things we did not need and spent a lot of money. My parents told me to return most of the items and get the money back.

At around that time, my father took me to see Dr. Nass again who strongly suggested I take *Lithium*. At that time, *Lithium* was the only medicine that could help control my mania along with the depression. Dr. Nass felt that it would be best to administer the drug in a hospital, since there was a lot of blood work to be done. I decided to give Lithium a chance. I went to *Hillside Hospital*, a part of *North Shore Long Island Jewish Medical Center*. This is a hospital that treats people with mental illness. My first night there was horrible. I did not feel comfortable because my roommate was not Jewish. Having a Jewish roommate was important to me because I liked to pray and I was kosher. Therefore, I needed someone who would understand my religious beliefs and customs. The next day, my father made sure that I would be in a room with someone who was Jewish.

At *Hillside*, the staff sat down with me and took notes of my history with bipolar disorder. They agreed with my doctor that I needed *Lithium*. Throughout the two weeks that I stayed in the hospital, I hated it because most of the patients had more serious problems than I did. Some were on drugs and smoked cigarettes. Each day that I was there, I looked forward to the day that I could go home and be with my family. However, there was one thing I liked at *Hillside Hospital* and that was the group meetings that I had with the other patients. It felt good to be around people who had similar diagnoses. It was nice to know that I was not alone because the groups made me understand how others with mental illness had bigger problems than the ones I had. Although I wanted to go home, I admit that meeting new people and making new friends gave me hope that one day I would recover from mental illness.

When I left *Hillside*, I went back to the *Advanced Center for Psychotherapy*. Although I was under the care of Dr. Nass, the clinic allowed me to continue to see him, as long as I came to see a therapist every week. My new therapist was very direct and strong minded. Once during a session, she noticed I was acting very peculiar and knew that I was in the beginning stages of developing another manic episode. This was at a time when I went to a party that Al hosted for singles. I felt euphoric and way too happy. My therapist contacted Dr. Nass and told her to tell me to take more milligrams of *Prolixin*, along with the *Lithium*. At that moment, I made an appointment to see Dr. Nass and he told me to start taking *Depakote*, an anticonvulsant mood stabilizer medication which was used to treat bipolar disorder and epilepsy. After taking *Depakote* for a few weeks, it helped stabilize my mood swings, whereby *Lithium* had no effect.

My psychiatrist wanted me to continue to take *Depakote* with the *Prolixin*. It helped clear my judgment and relieve me from some of the hallucinations that I had and voices that I heard in my head. Dr. Nass also gave me *Cogentin* which helped with muscle movements and which is a side effect one gets from taking *Prolixin*. It is one of the oldest medications that, to this very day, has worked miraculously for me and still does. As a result of these medications I took, the manic symptoms I had did not come back. I did not hear any more voices or have hallucinations. I was not euphoric anymore. Never again did I go on a shopping spree and my judgment was getting back to normal.

While I was battling my manic depression, my grandmother died at the age of eighty-eight. During the five years that she lived with us, we all got closer to her. Near the end, we took her to a hospice because it was hard for my mother to take care of her. I wanted to go to see her but I could not because there was a singles party that same night. I had thought it was more important for me to meet someone than to see my grandmother who was dying. Afterwards,

I felt guilty because I should have gone with them. By morning, she passed away and I went with my parents and saw her lifeless. Again, I was afraid for my mother, but also for myself because of the mental illnesses that we both had. My grandmother's death was hard on all of us, but it was also a relief because she was no longer suffering.

After this, I continued to see my therapist at the *Advanced Center for Psychotherapy*. She helped me come to terms with my illness, let go of Al, and solve many of the problems that I had with my family. However, I was still unhappy. I had problems building relationships, which posed difficulties in my romantic endeavors. I often talked with my therapist about this and she said to me, "When it is right, you will know". At that time, I did not want someone with a mental illness, since there was enough of it in my family. I knew that there was a lot of stigma towards the mentally ill and I took a risk when I told friends that I suffered from bipolar disorder. Every time I dated someone new, I felt I should be honest with them. However, once I said something about my mental illness, they would run away from me and would not care about the other good qualities I had. This made me realize how much stigma there is in the world.

I became very fearful of the outside world because I did not know how others would respond to me. You are often judged by your illness rather than as a *person* who has an illness. Soon I realized that I may have to look for someone to be with who suffered from a mental illness. I asked my therapist why this would be easier on me and she told me that I would not have to worry about the stigma when it came to dating a person with mental illness, and that there would be understanding and communication, since we shared the same pain, strife, and sense of emotional disconnection with others.

As a result of being diagnosed with bipolar disorder, I had a lot of challenges to face besides those in the dating world. I also feared going back to work. In the next few chapters, I will discuss these challenges and how recovery was possible.

CHAPTER FIVE
GETTING BACK TO WORK

Having bipolar disorder, I had fears of how others would respond to me in the workplace. It was a struggle for me. Every time I had a job interview I became nervous because of the stigma associated with having a mental illness. I was far too open with the interviewer about my illness and that was a mistake. In the business world, companies do not know who you are and sometimes discriminate if there is something wrong with you, mentally or physically.

After my hospitalization, it became more difficult to find work. My father suggested I apply for Social Security Disability Insurance (*SSDI*). Applying for government benefits was not an easy task. The first time I went to Social Security there were long lines which caused me to wait until my number was called. When my number was finally called, the clerk gave me an application form to fill out. When I finished the application, it was mailed to Social Security, and within weeks I received an answer. It stated that although I had difficulty in stressful situations, based on my age and education, I could perform a job with simple tasks. What Social Security did not understand was that accommodations are necessary in order for a mentally ill person to get a job and keep it, depending on the severity of that person's illness. They do not realize how stressful job interviews can be, why disclosure is so difficult, and how it is a struggle to maintain a job in today's changing technology. This was before they developed the *Ticket to Work* program.

After I received the first rejection letter, I filed another application form for reconsideration. This time Social Security recognized that although I had bipolar disorder which caused difficulty in concentrating and relating to people, they still felt I could do a job with simple tasks. I asked myself, "How could they say this to me when they know I have a severe mental illness? How can a person work when they suffer from issues, problems, stigma, and discrimination due to their mental illness?"

I thought my battle with Social Security was a lost cause until I was advised to see a lawyer. The first thing I had to do was file a request for a hearing so a judge could examine my case. When I saw the judge, he saw how nervous I was and how difficult it was to express myself. Finally, after two weeks, I received a letter from the judge which stated that I would get my Social Security Disability benefits and Medicare. My family was so proud of me because of the amount of work I had put into getting these benefits. I was going to get the income and health insurance that I desperately needed.

After I received Social Security Disability, my father helped me get a job at Touro College since he knew the president. It was not much of a job, but it helped build my self esteem. I was hired as a secretary to the operations manager at *Dov Revel*, a part of Touro College in Forest Hills, Queens. I was content at Touro and knew that I was not going to be fired for my mental illness because the president had done this as a favor to my father. This job helped me get back into the workplace.

During my time at Touro, I studied medical billing at Queens College. Again, I was not sure if this field was for me, but I was glad to complete the course and received a certificate in medical billing. When my job at Touro was terminated due to budget cuts, I was not depressed, but at the same time was nervous and excited about looking for a job as a medical biller. I was nervous because I was afraid that I would have another relapse.

One time, I found a job as a medical secretary, but the doctor noticed I was not well mentally because I made too many mistakes, so he fired me.

I realized I needed help and support in getting a job and keeping it. My therapist recommended that I go to *VESID* (Vocational and Educational Services for Individuals with Disabilities) for assistance. The first time I saw a counselor at *VESID*, he put me in touch with a supported employment program that is associated with *Hillside Hospital*. It was there that I learned how to type a resume, how to interview for a job, and whether or not to disclose my mental illness.

At that time, I was hired as a medical biller for a company that assisted doctors in getting their patients to pay bills for their services. My job coach spoke to my supervisor and told him I had a disability so that he would not fire me. However, I had a lot of trouble adjusting to this type of work. It was my duty to get the patients to pay their bills, but I was not very assertive with them. This was also a money-making business and I did not enjoy being in such a cut throat environment. Each day that I came to work, I cried and confessed to my job coach that this was not the right job for me. She begged me to stay, but I could not handle it, so I quit. I knew this would jeopardize my relationship with the agency and therefore left the program at *Hillside Hospital.*

Eventually, I decided to take a year off from working in the business world and do some volunteering. I found a volunteer job with the *New York City Public School Volunteer Program.* I volunteered for a school in Forest Hills as a teacher's assistant or paraprofessional. I liked the work so much that my whole face was beaming. I tutored first graders and assisted the teacher when she needed me. For example, I once led the class while she went to get something, and the students listened respectively and attentively. This made me believe that teaching would be one of the vocations that I would seek employment in.

After one year of volunteering, I applied for a paraprofessional position at my district in Forest Hills, but there were no openings. The Board of Education dealt with special needs kids and they were hiring at that district. Although I had no experience with this type of population, I substituted at several schools and dealt with children who were developmentally disabled, mentally retarded, and autistic. This line of work was tough on me and I soon realized that this area of education was not for me, so I left the system. Quitting my jobs as a medical biller and substitute teacher made me realize how low my self esteem was in these fields. I had to look for something that dealt with a certain culture or population that was not as difficult to handle and would increase my self confidence.

A few months later, I went back to *VESID* and they recommended another supported employment program called *Transitional Services of New York*. This program helped me a lot. The vocational counselor assigned me to a job coach and a job developer. The job coach assisted me with my resume and interviewing skills. The job developer helped me by looking into job leads so she could explain to the employer what the agency was all about. This helped me because the employer then knew I had a disability, but was willing to work with my job coach so I could keep the job. This agency was far better than the one at *Hillside Hospital*. I also believed that this agency started my journey of recovery in the workplace.

My job coach at *Transitional Services of New York* assisted me with some leads for clerical work. One lead was in a hardware store, but I did not like it because I was alone and lacked supervision. I also came up with job leads on my own. Once, a friend of mine told me that Bramson Ort College was hiring tutors so I sent my resume, was interviewed, and was hired immediately. I notified my job coach and followed up with her in the event I had any problems at work and in order to keep the job.

The job at Bramson Ort College was the first stable job I had had in a long time. At first, I was hired as an ESL tutor where I was given a caseload of five students who were foreign to the English language. I used the curriculum books that the tutoring department had so I could teach the students how to read, write, and speak English in various situations. After four months as an ESL tutor, Bramson Ort decided to hire me as a clerical assistant to the students and faculty. I notified *Transitional Services of New York* and decided to disclose my disability. I did a variety of work for them. Some of my duties were filing, copying, faxing, data entry, and researching on the internet.

I also helped prepare for special events, such as *Women's and Black History Month*. I even organized my own event at the college for *Mental Illness Awareness Month*. Since *Transitional Services of New York* guided me so much in getting this job, I arranged to have a speaker address the services they had to offer for individuals with mental illness. I also brought a videotape called, "Moving Back into the Light." This video was about overcoming depression.

While working at Bramson Ort, I decided to do some volunteer activities that advocated for individuals with mental illness. I became involved with *New York City Voices*, a newspaper for those with mental illness. One of the first articles that I wrote for this publication was titled, "*My Fears in Overcoming Bipolar Disorder.*" The article described my illness, fears I had in building relationships, and going back to work. I was thrilled and excited to have this article published. This article also helped people come out and share their stories with the public. At that time, I had no idea that this article would be the catalyst in building my career in mental health.

Another volunteer activity I organized was to host an event at my synagogue, *Havurat Yisrael*, about stigma towards the mentally ill. To my knowledge, this was one of the first events on mental illness held in an orthodox congregation. It was important for me to educate the orthodox community because some are quite biased and are less accepting of people with mental illness. To do this, I arranged for three speakers from *Community Access*, an agency that helps people with psychiatric disabilities, to talk about stigma towards the mentally ill. The three speakers were Kathy Berke, Marty Cohen, and Robin Simon.

Kathy Berke spoke about her recovery from bipolar disorder and her position as a job developer for one of their clubhouses. This clubhouse offered services such as housing and employment to people recovering from mental illness. She stated that there is a "double edged sword" surrounding stigma and treatment meaning that those with mental illness are afraid to seek treatment because they fear society will shun them for opening up. Ms. Berke also said that some Chassidic Jews felt intense shame in being mentally ill. So much emphasis is placed on achievement and intellectual pursuits that it keeps people in the closet.

Marty Cohen, a consumer advocate, spoke about his suffering from obsessive compulsive disorder for 30 years before being diagnosed. He also had clients who were very religious Jews and members of *Community Access*. Mr. Cohen stated that the media often misleads the public concerning the myths and realities of mental illness.

The importance of supported employment was also a big issue at this event. The event addressed the flaws within the *Americans for Disabilities Act*, such as allowing employers to discriminate in hiring the mentally ill. Robin Simon, a consumer advocate, stated that employers need to understand that individuals with mental illness need accommodations in the workplace such as more breaks and having a quiet room to concentrate in.

This event was so important to me that I called the *Jewish Week*, a newspaper for Jews who want to know what is going on inside and outside their community. I spoke to the editorial intern and invited her to come with a photographer. It was my first publicity event. In the article, she mentioned the struggles and symptoms that I went through with bipolar disorder. She also wrote how I felt about stigma and how important it was to educate synagogues in order to help those Jews who suffered from mental illness and thus lost their faith in Judaism and in God.

When I worked at Bramson Ort College, I became involved with *NAMI*, which stands for the National Alliance for Mentally Ill. I met a woman at one of their events who worked at *Holliswood Hospital* in Queens and who asked me to speak in a panel discussion about my recovery from mental illness. I never spoke in public before which made me a little bit nervous. I decided to do it because it would be educational for individuals, families, and professionals dealing with mental health issues. The crowd liked hearing my story because it helped them to understand what mental health means to those who struggle with it every day, whether at work, in school, or in one's family.

As a result, I did not know that these activities would be the start of developing a career in mental health and learning to deal with other challenges ahead which could affect my own mental health treatment.

CHAPTER SIX

STRUGGLING TO FIND A MATE AND CARING FOR A LOVED ONE

In chapter four, I spoke about how finding the right man was difficult because I suffered from bipolar disorder (manic depression). Men did not want to date me once they found out about my mental illness. Some men were even scared to be around me because they worried about what their parents would say if they were dating a girl with a mental illness.

Once, I dated a man who was sweet, kind, and honest and was looking for those same qualities in a woman. We went out a few times, and on the fifth date I told him that I had bipolar disorder, a mental illness. He seemed to understand at first, but when we went away for a weekend getaway, he wanted to stay up late one night and I told him I was tired and had to take my medications. He was so annoyed and told me to "forget about my pills." I left him and went upstairs to the room and cried my heart out. All his understanding about my mental illness was a lie. The next morning, he told me that this was new to him and that he was scared about how his parents would react to someone with a disease like this. This was unfair to me and therefore, I ended the relationship with him. As a result, I needed to find someone who dealt with mental illness, just like me.

My therapist suggested that I become a member of the National Alliance for Mentally Ill, known as *NAMI*, an organization that advocates for people with mental illness. They have meetings once a month to educate families who have a spouse, son, daughter, or sibling with a mental illness. *NAMI* also publishes a newsletter that is issued every two months so that the community can be informed.

My therapist also told me that they have something called *The Friendship Network*, as explained in chapter one. Alice Cohen, who runs *The Friendship Network*, told me that it was not a matchmaking service, but a place where you can meet others who suffer from mental illness like me. I decided to become a member, but told Alice that I only wanted to meet Jewish people. She said it was possible, but that it was also opened to anyone of a different race, religion, or ethnic group. I dated a few people from the *Friendship Network*, but it did not work out so I decided to keep them as acquaintances. However, I met two girls, both Jewish, that I have remained friends with until this day. One of them got married and had three children. The other remained single and is dating a man she met through the *Friendship Network*. I also joined in many of their social activities. I played tennis, bowled, went to barbecue picnics they had in the summer, attended support groups, and went to some conferences that were discounted because I was a member. The *Friendship Network* helped me regain my social life and taught me how to disclose my illness outside the community. As a result, I did not meet enough Jewish people, so when I became strong enough to deal with people in the Jewish community, I left the *Friendship Network*.

When I left Alice Cohen's *Friendship Network*, I decided to meet people through my synagogue, *Havurat Yisrael*. The rabbi at my temple ran some programs for singles with the help of a matchmaker. I met some nice people, and even dated some who were religious, but I had other problems in relating to people.

Once, at *Havurat Yisrael*, I met this man who wanted to set me up with his friend who lived in Brooklyn. I gave him my number and his friend called me the next day. His name was Charles Katz. I had no idea that he would turn out to be the best loving husband in the world.

While I waited for him to pick me up for our first date, I looked out the window of my apartment and saw him walking towards my building. I noticed how thin he was and that he had a mustache, which I did not like. While walking to *Empire Roasters* restaurant with him, he looked very nervous because his arm was bent and shaky. We talked about how being orthodox Jews and visits to Israel were important parts of our lives. We also discussed the movies and music we liked and what we did for a living. As you can see, Charles and I had a lot in common. After we ate, we walked to the park, and for some reason I felt there was something wrong with him on the inside. He wanted to ask me out again for a second date, but I told him I would think about it. Charles looked sad, but I wanted to become friends with him, so I asked for his phone number.

A month later, Charles called me and we went out again. This was our second date. This time, Charles gave me some presents which must have cost him a lot of money. I spoke to my parents about this who felt I should mail the gifts back to him, and I did. The next day, he called my mother and apologized to her for coming with presents when I was not yet ready for a serious relationship.

From that day on, I knew he was serious about me, but things were moving too fast, so we decided to remain friends.

Two years later, Havurat Yisrael had a singles *Shabbaton* (a social group meeting on the Sabbath) where I met Charles again. After having dinner with him that Friday night I asked him to walk me home because it was dark and cold. As we walked, he told me that he had moved out of his parents' home and had rented a basement apartment from another family. He worked full time at an advertising agency as a proofreader. At the *Shabbaton*, I mentioned that I was planning an event about mental illness at the synagogue. Charles seemed happy to learn that I also had a mental illness. I told him I was diagnosed with bipolar disorder at the age of twenty-four. He told me that after he moved out from his parents' house, he became mentally ill, so his parents took him to the *Jewish Board of Family and Children's Services* where he was diagnosed with major depression. Charles told me about some of the symptoms he had. He used to think people were coming after him when he heard voices in his head. I understood what Charles was going through since I had similar symptoms. It was then that I started to like him, but still did not want to date him seriously because of the fear that if we ever married and had children, they might develop a mental illness later in life. As for me, it was a good feeling to have someone out there who understood my situation.

We dated on and off for five years. During this time, I went out with other people, but none of them understood my illness the way Charles did. It was then that I was struggling with the thought of whether Charles was the right man for me in life. He was sensitive, kind, funny, and cute. Charles was also someone I could share problems with that came up with my family. It was not until tragedy struck my family again, that I wanted to get into a serious relationship with Charles. I knew that he was the only man in the whole world that really liked me. I decided to get up the courage and ask him if he wanted to date me. Charles was very happy that I made this decision to ask him. We finally found each other and got serious.

While Charles and I were dating, he wanted me to meet his sister and her husband, so we all met at a restaurant. His sister seemed nice but her husband seemed strange to me, as if he also had something wrong with him. When Charles took me home, I told him that he was not mature enough for me to date on a serious level. The real reason I broke up with him was because I did not like his brother-in-law, which I now realize is not a good reason to break up with someone when you are in love.

After Charles and I broke up, he kept sending me flowers, hoping that I would come back to him. He even sent a romantic letter to me by Federal Express which must have cost him a lot of money. It was also his way of apologizing to me, even though he had not done anything wrong. It was I who left him. That week, I went to a singles party and asked myself, "What is wrong with me? Charles loves me and I love him. Why should I care about what kind of family he is from? If I really like him, I should be able to get along with his brother-in-law. Will Charles forgive me and take me back?" It took one week to get back together with him. The flowers he sent me made me see how much he cared for me and missed me. I missed him too, so I called him one Saturday night and told him how sorry I was and that I still loved him. As a result, we started dating again and were serious about one another.

Although this was a happy time for me, it was a very sad one too. In June 2001, my mother got sick. While my father was out, my mother wanted me to do some food shopping for her. As lazy as I am sometimes, I told her I was too tired. I did not know how sick she was and when my father came home, he scolded me because I acted so selfishly. If I had known she was that sick, I would have helped her. I live with that regret every day of my life.

My mother had developed a fever of over 102° and went to see her primary care physician who did a blood test. It showed that her white blood cell count was extremely high and that she was anemic. The doctor contacted an oncologist and sent her to *Mount Sinai Hospital* in New York.

When my father told me we had to take my mother to the hospital, I was shocked. I thought it was only a fever and that she would get better, but that was not the case. My father drove and when we got to the hospital, I took over and parked the car in a parking lot, while my father helped her to get admitted to a room on the sixth floor where there were other patients suffering from cancer. After parking the car, I went to her room and waited with my father until her blood tests came back. We met with the oncologist who told us that my mother had leukemia, a cancer of the blood. It was then that I was afraid for my mother thinking she may not be able to fight this disease and may lose her life, which my father and I did not want to see happen. My father and I kept giving her hope and tried to remain strong and positive for her throughout this illness, but we all knew it would be only a matter of time, because nobody I have ever known had survived cancer.

I was under a lot of stress from work and in caring for my beloved mother. I needed to seek another psychiatrist who was closer in proximity to me. I spoke to my psychiatrist, Dr. Nass, and told him that I had to leave him and switch to a psychiatrist at the *Advanced Center for Psychotherapy*, where I saw my therapist. This made sense because in that way, the psychiatrist and therapist could communicate with each other about my mental health, and which was something the clinic definitely wanted. I will always be grateful to Dr. Nass because he was the one that helped me from the start with my mental illness.

Since I had mental illness, I thought I was going to get sicker and more depressed because I could not handle the fact that my mother might slip away from me because she had leukemia. I was glad I continued to see my psychiatrist and therapist because I worried about my mother and had doubts as to whether I could deal with such a crisis. It was then that Dr. Blair Skolnick prescribed *Wellbutrin* for me, an antidepressant, which would make me feel less awful than I was already feeling.

While my mother was in the hospital, I started dating Charles on an even more serious level. It was good to have someone so special on my side throughout all this. My mother was so happy to hear that I was dating Charles because she wanted to think about something else other than her illness. One important thing that she told me was to stay with Charles and not to break up with him again. This meant so much to my mother and to me too because Charles was the kind of man that had a loving golden heart and my mother knew that this was what I needed in my life.

My mother's oncologist told us that she had to have at least four cycles of chemotherapy to cure her cancer. I was so scared that she might die and would not live to see me get married. When she started her first cycle of chemotherapy, I began to see changes with her body such as losing her hair and appetite, needing help taking a shower or a bath, and becoming more depressed. I had to take off from work so I could visit her in the hospital and help her at home. My father and I ended up celebrating her 63rd birthday at *Mount Sinai Hospital*. We brought her a cake and decorated the room for her, and everybody said happy birthday to her, even the nurses and the rest of staff who worked there. She was never so happy. However, little did we know that this would be her last birthday.

After the first cycle of chemotherapy was over, she was able to go home, but the oncologist wanted her to undergo three more cycles of chemotherapy. I was thinking, how could my mother handle such treatments? My father and I took her to *New York Hospital of Queens* to undergo the remaining cycles of chemotherapy. This was done in between the Jewish holidays of *Rosh Hashanah*, *Yom Kippur*, and *Succoth*, which we celebrated. When she was done with the fourth cycle, she went home where she received help from a home health aide and a nurse, because my father, and especially me, could not give her injections. I become afraid, nervous, and anxious when I am not sure what to do.

After the treatments were finished, I went with my mother to see the oncologist who gave us some good news. My mother's cancer was gone and was in remission. My father and I were so happy that my mother was getting better, and for two months she went back to her daily activities.

At that time, she saw how much I liked Charles and wanted to meet him again. I decided to introduce him to my parents and they were both happy, not just because I found someone, but because he was a person that could relate to my mental illness, since he also had one.

Life was happy for me again. I found the right man who was able to listen, care, and understand me. Having him in my life at this time gave me some comfort in the situation with my mother. Knowing that her cancer was gone was also very good for us because my father and I wanted her to live a long life so she could see me get married and have children some day. However, deep down in my heart, I had a dreadful feeling that her life was not going to last much longer. The thought of that made me feel very dark inside.

Life is precious and has its ups and downs. Sometimes you have to adapt and be strong. Life is also a test, especially, when you are facing a crisis. Being someone with a mental illness, I know how life can change in ways I would never expect.

CHAPTER 7

THE DEATH OF MY MOTHER

Charles started coming over to the house a lot. On *Chanukah* my mother made potato pancakes for him and he liked the hospitality my parents offered him. He was beginning to feel like he was a part of the family.

One day, my mother developed a fever again and saw some brown spots appearing on her body. We hoped that she would get better. On that day, Charles came over and told us that his mother had gall bladder cancer, but was in the early stages of her cancer. He wanted my mother to know that she was not alone in fighting this battle of cancer.

Two days later, my parents made an appointment with the oncologist who told my mother that the leukemia had come back and that she would have to go to *Mount Sinai Hospital* again. This time my cousin Sharon, with whom I had a very, very close relationship, was here to drive them to the hospital and I felt exhausted and emotionally weak. I went to visit her the very next day. The dreadful feeling that I had came back, and even though the doctors and nurses did not tell us, I knew in my heart that my mother was dying. That weekend, I decided to spend the Sabbath with her at the hospital. An organization called *Bikur Cholim*, which helps people who want to be with their loved ones when they are sick, let me stay in one of the apartments they had in the city. When I told Charles that my mother's cancer came back and that she was in the hospital again, he wanted to be with me that weekend. Although I was feeling very depressed, his staying with me was a lot of comfort. It was then that I really fell in love with him.

On that Sabbath, my father also came to visit her. She was hooked up to a machine to decrease the white blood cell count from her body. I did not like *Mount Sinai*. There was a shortage of nurses and sometimes I felt nervous, anxious and numb because I did not know how to help my mother. Sometimes my mother would get up from bed and go to the bathroom by herself where she would play with the intravenous tube and let blood come out, whenever she fell on the floor. The nurses were slow and could not watch her twenty-four hours a day, so my father requested that she should have someone stay in her room day and night. I never felt so helpless in all my life.

The week after I made plans with my cousin Sharon to visit my mother on a Sunday morning. We were supposed to leave at eleven o'clock in the morning. Sharon had a friend visiting her when we were supposed to leave and all of a sudden, I got upset because of the long time I had to wait. All I thought about was my mother and that she was expecting us. I knew my cousin was also upset, which is probably why she needed to have a friend there. Having company over was her way of dealing with my mother's illness. I was getting impatient, angry, and depressed because my mother was waiting for us and Sharon did not listen to me. When Sharon came over, we fought about why she was so late. My father lost his patience and yelled at us saying, "Your mother is dying!" Hearing those words actually spoken made me so unhappy that for the first time I realized the truth. My mother was going to be taken from us very soon.

My cousin Sharon and I finally got to the hospital in the afternoon. When we visited my mother, she wondered what had taken us so long to get there. Sharon and I just told her it was because of traffic. We did not want to upset her by telling her the real reason. Then my mother asked me a very bleak question and I did not know what to answer her. She said, "I felt as if I was going to die last night. Am I dying?" I responded by telling her that she must keep fighting and not think thoughts like that, even though my cousin Sharon and I knew it was a lie.

During this time, my mother's oncologist experimented with another type of chemotherapy that affected all of the cells in her body, especially the kidneys. One time when I visited her, I noticed she had difficulty breathing. At this point, I was really scared that I would lose my mother so I called my therapist at the *Advanced Center for Psychotherapy* about what was happening. If I did not continue with my psychiatric treatment, who knows what would have happened to me. Maybe the voices and the euphoria symptoms I experienced when I was manic would return as well as my depression. I was content that my psychiatrist and therapist were there for support. They gave me strength so that I would be able to cope and know what to do should my mother pass away.

That evening while my father and I were at home, a nurse called to inform us that the situation with my mother was getting worse.

The doctors and nurses on staff wanted to put her on a respirator, but her proxy stated that she did not want to be hooked up to a machine. Even though it was the Sabbath, my father drove us to the hospital, and when we got there, my father came to the decision to put her on life support. After all, my mother was only sixty-three. She was taken to the intensive care unit, and we went there with her.

That Monday night, my father and I received a call from the hospital telling us to be prepared and get ready to make arrangements for a funeral and burial. I went to the hospital after work and stayed there overnight, but there was no change in her condition. My father brought all the papers that were needed and rushed to the hospital the next morning. When he arrived, my father and I watched her slip away bit by bit. I could even feel her arms getting ice cold. I had to be brave and accept the fact that my mother was dying. As she slipped away, I wanted to cry and tell her, "Please, don't die, I need you!" but instead I comforted her and said, "God has a purpose for you in heaven and you will see your parents soon." The rabbi who was at the hospital and my father recited some special prayers for her so she would be at peace. At about 3:19 p.m. on Tuesday, February 12, 2002, my mother died. The physicians and nurses that were on duty told us how sorry they were that they could not keep her alive even with the respirator attached to her. Every bone in my body wanted to cry, scream and blame the staff which was in the intensive care unit for not keeping her alive. I did not want to fall into a relapse because my father needed me to be in a good mental state after my mother's death.

My father and I made arrangements for the funeral and burial. While at *Mount Sinai Hospital*, my father called *Adath Yisrael* to take away the body so that it could be washed and cleaned for the funeral and burial. Before they took my mother away, I went to say good-bye one last time, kissing her even though she was unable to feel it. When we left for home, I made calls to our friends and relatives to tell them what happened while my father went to the rabbi at my temple, *Havurat Yisrael*, and to the funeral parlor to discuss the arrangements. Charles, the first person that I called, decided to take off from work just to be with me. Even though I knew he could not be near the body because of religious reasons and customs, I was glad that he was around to comfort me and pay his respects.

The funeral was held at *Schwartz Brothers* in Forest Hills, Queens. Before it started, my father and I were asked to identify the body. When I saw my mother's face, I could not look at her, so I turned away. Rabbi Algaze tore our shirts, a Jewish custom performed when an immediate family member dies. I cried to my best friend Deena who comforted me when Charles could not. I called the *Advanced Center for Psychotherapy* to tell my therapist that my mother passed away and to tell her where the funeral was going to be. To my surprise, my therapist came to the funeral and paid her respects to me. I was glad that she came because she had prepared me emotionally throughout all of this. My therapist told me that I had every right to be depressed because this was my mother that I had loved and known all my life.

At the funeral where the service was held, everybody stood up when we entered the room. Rabbi Algaze spoke kind words about my mother; how her life was a struggle fighting mental illness and cancer, and that she raised a wonderful daughter in the Jewish faith. I could not speak because it was too emotional for me. My father was too stressed out from all the work involved in arranging the funeral and burial. The greatest thing my mother taught me was how to survive in today's society.

After the funeral was over, my father rented a limousine and we went to *Beth Moses Cemetery* in Farmingdale, New York so she could finally be put to rest in her burial place. When Rabbi Algaze said some prayers, and as my mother's body was being put to rest, I sobbed. Throughout all this, I was afraid of having another mental relapse and knew I needed to continue with my treatment so I would be healthy and strong for my father, which was all I had left.

After the burial, my father and I went home to sit *shiva*, (a Jewish custom observed for seven days when there is a death of a close relative). When I came home, Charles was there waiting for me. Every night that he came over, I was comforted. One time when he came over, I looked at his face and was surprised that he shaved off his mustache. I hugged and kissed him in front of everybody, but I realized this was not appropriate for a mourner to do. Charles stayed with friends in the neighborhood so he could come and spend the Sabbath with me during the *shiva* for my mother. Many of our relatives and friends came to pay their respects and to comfort us by bringing food so we would not have to cook. This is a Jewish custom which was really nice and also a *mitzvah* (a good deed) they did.

I had a very good support system in that my family, friends, psychiatrist and therapist were there for me during this tough time in my life. This helped me with my recovery from bipolar disorder. It was important to me that I continue to live a life that my mother wanted for me. I know that the loss of my mother will always remain within me, but her death proved that I was able to overcome a major loss in my life.

CHAPTER 8
RECOVERY AFTER LOSS

It was very difficult to recover from the death of my mother. When the *shiva* for my mother was over, it was hard for me to get adjusted to the fact that she would never be in my life again. My father and I gave away all her clothes to the Salvation Army. As I went through her clothes, I started to feel depressed, but also thought that some of her dresses might fit me since we were the same weight. I thought that wearing her dresses would be a great way to remember her, especially if I wore the dresses on Sabbath.

My mother's death was even harder for my father because they shared the same bedroom for so many years. He had to make some changes like getting rid of the queen sized bed that they had slept in. He had to get to know where things were in the kitchen. For instance, knowing which silverware was used for dairy or for meat, learning how to cook again, doing the laundry, and ironing his clothes. The fact that I was still living with him helped a lot. When he did not know what kind of food to buy, I often went with him to the supermarket and showed him where certain foods and beverages were located. Without my help, the loss of my mother would have been an even greater burden for him.

Once things got back to normal, I went back to work at Bramson Ort College and started to date Charles and we got even more serious. I finally met his parents who told me how sorry they were to hear about my mother's death. At this meeting, I learned that his mother's cancer had spread and she told me how good it felt to see that her son was so happy with me. She hugged and kissed me, as if she approved of me on some level. I now felt like I had another family.

Not long after meeting his parents, Passover arrived. I wanted to invite Charles but my father wanted to be alone with me. When my mother was alive, she had done all the cooking, arranged the *seder* plate, (a special plate containing symbolic foods eaten or displayed at the Passover seder) and often invited other people. However, because my mother passed away, my father didn't want anyone else to be there. We decided to order food catered by Mauzone, a store in Queens that sells kosher food. I remembered how my mother arranged the *seder* plate, so I bought all the things that were needed such as the egg, horseradish, parsley, and shank bone. It was a quiet Passover for us that year, but we managed to get through it.

A couple of weeks after Passover, Charles told me that his mother was in the hospital again because of her cancer. He asked me if I wanted to visit her but I was not sure because it would have brought back sad thoughts about when my own mother was in the hospital. I decided to go anyway and met his father, sister and her husband there. However, I could not stay in the room because it became too emotional for me. Before I left the room, I promised Charles's mother that I would always take good care of her son. I knew that she did not have long to live, which is why Charles brought me to see her. He needed comfort and since I went through the same situation with my own mother, he felt better knowing that I understood.

After this, Charles and I discussed marriage. On Sunday, June 9, 2002, Charles parked his car on a street close to my home and proposed to me with an engagement ring that once belonged to his grandmother. When his mother was moved to a nursing home, she gave Charles her last wish, which was to give his grandmother's ring to me. It was the most sentimental thing that Charles ever did, and I accepted it.

After we had dinner, Charles and I went to my father and told him about our engagement. We were all happy until my father mentioned that he wanted Charles and me to sign a prenuptial agreement. My father never trusted people with our money, and because my name was on certain accounts, he wanted to protect his investments. Charles was very upset that I did not tell him about this, but my father had asked me not to, which I now think was a mistake. Charles almost ran out the door and I thought this was going to be the end for us. Knowing that Charles's anger was tied to his mental illness, my father and I begged him to stay so we could talk about this rationally. I knew that Charles did not have knowledge about investments so my father asked Charles to call his father and talk to him. Charles's father told him not to make a big deal about this, and explained to him what my father wanted. Charles understood and started to calm down. At this point, Charles agreed to go ahead with what my father wanted because it was the only way he could marry me and receive my father's blessing.

On June 17, 2002, *Havurat Yisrael*, the synagogue that I belonged to, was going to make an announcement of my engagement to Charles. I invited him to spend the weekend with my family and me so he could be here for this. However, Charles's mother was in bad shape and I could tell that something was on his mind. The next day, his father, sister and her husband came to discuss wedding arrangements with my father and me. We discussed that the wedding should be in *Temple Torah* because of the close connection my Aunt Bertha had with the synagogue. We also talked about seating arrangements and the type of music and photographer we wanted. Charles asked his family about his mother's prognosis, since they had just come back from visiting her. His sister told him that she was worse than ever and that he should visit her again for what would have been the last time, or so we thought.

That evening, his landlord made a *"vort,"* (the Jewish or Yiddish word for an engagement party) in honor of our engagement. Our families were invited and there was food, dancing and music. Many of the people who came were very religious orthodox Jews, and a few of them were Chasidim. It was different from what my family and I had ever experienced, since we basically grew up as conservative Jews, but everybody had a great time.

The next morning, I received a phone call from Charles at about seven o'clock telling me that his mother passed away. My only regret was that he should have spent that weekend with his mother instead of being with me. I told my father what happened and the next day we went to the funeral home in Flatbush, Brooklyn. For all the times that Charles was there for my mother, I felt that the least I could do was be there for him too. Charles was and is the love of my life and therefore, I feared that his depression would get worse after the death of his mother. At the funeral, I met many of his relatives, especially his aunts, uncles, and cousins. They were very pleased to meet me even though it was a very sad occasion. After the funeral, my father drove us back to Queens where the burial was to take place. We had arrived there a little late but made it in time for the service. Because Charles practiced a religious custom, he could not go to other people's funerals or burials, but when it came to his mother's, he had to be there with the rest of his family. I realized how special his mother had been because she had raised a wonderful, kind hearted, loving son.

After the *shiva* period for his mother, Charles went back to work and we started making plans for our wedding. It was a hard time for both our families because we had lost our mothers within the same year. We still had to go on living our lives because that is what our parents wanted for us.

In August 2002, I lost my job at Bramson Ort College due to budget cuts so I decided to concentrate on our wedding plans and look for other things to do with my time. I became a member of *Venture House*, a clubhouse for those with mental illness that offers its members a place where they can belong, and the opportunity to volunteer in various departments, such as housing, employment, and administration. I was interested in volunteering in the employment unit but was not ready to commit to them. I helped out with little things such as writing short articles, developing resumes, taking staff meeting minutes, and sending out birthday cards. It was nice and very special. *Venture House* made me feel as if I was part of a community. They played a big part in my recovery, not just from mental illness, but they also helped me to move on with my life. Coming to *Venture House* and planning a wedding kept me busy, which helped me recover from feeling the sadness in knowing that my mother was gone.

When *Rosh Hashanah* and *Yom Kippur* came, it was difficult for both our families, since this was the first Jewish New Year without our mothers. I decided to pray at the main sanctuary with my father at the *Forest Hills Jewish Center* because this would be the last time we would spend there together as a family. Everything was changing. Charles and I had found an apartment in Kew Gardens Hills, a Jewish area where many orthodox Jews live, and I was getting married and in the process of moving to my own apartment with Charles.

Planning our wedding put us under a lot of pressure. We had to get our invitations out, decide on the music we wanted, set up the seating arrangements for the dinner, and finish the prenuptial agreement that needed to be signed by Charles and me. Although it was a hectic time for us, it was all worth it because Charles and I knew we would be happy together. Having a wedding the same year in which we were still in mourning for both our mothers was something I knew our mothers would not object to. They would want us to be happy and not always be sad and depressed because they were no longer with us.

The day of our wedding, Sunday, November 10, 2002, was soon approaching. My cousin Sharon had planned a surprise bridal shower for me at *Chosen Garden*, a kosher Chinese restaurant. I knew deep down something was going on, but did not know what it was. That morning, my father was concerned about what I was wearing for my date with Charles, so he told me to change from pants into a skirt. Charles had seen me in pants before so I had wondered what the big problem was. I did not ask my father, so I just changed my clothes and went on my date with Charles. I knew we were going out to *Chosen Garden*, but I thought it was going to be like any other date we had. When we arrived, I saw some relatives, friends, and his sister, and I never looked more surprised than I did on that day. My cousin Sharon had arranged all the flowers and decorations which made the place beautiful. One by one I opened up all the gifts that would be used for my new home. When we finished eating, my father and his father came over and we took some pictures. I never thought I would be so happy in my entire life. After the bridal shower was over, I thanked everyone for all the gifts they had bought for me. As it turned out, it was a great day.

Two weeks before our wedding, we had the *auf ruf* (a Jewish custom performed a week before the wedding where you are called up to the Torah). It took place at Charles's synagogue, the *Seaview Jewish Center*, which was in his home town of Canarsie, Brooklyn. Both our families came and his father led the service. Rabbi Solomon gave a wonderful sermon and made a special blessing for us. At the *auf ruf*, Charles's father made sure that my father received an *aliyah* (the honor of being called up to bless the Torah). Charles read the *Maftir*, (a portion of the Torah reading) and then said the *Haftarah* (a short selection from the Prophets read in a synagogue every Sabbath following a reading from the Torah). After services were finished, Charles's father sponsored the *kiddush* (food and beverages served either at home or at a synagogue) and everyone congratulated us.

Our wedding day, Sunday, November 10, 2002, arrived. Charles and I never felt more nervous in our lives. I had to wake up at 5:30

in the morning to get my hair and makeup done which took almost two hours to do. I had my hair done in an up-do. After this, my father picked me up and drove me to *Temple Torah* in Little Neck, Queens where the wedding was to take place. In my mind, I wondered how Charles was getting along. If I was that uptight, I could imagine how Charles must have been feeling. I went to the bridal room so I could get dressed in my wedding gown. My cousin was the maid of honor and Charles's sister and my best friend were the bridesmaids. My father came in and saw how beautiful I looked, gave me a kiss and said to me, "Your mother would have been so proud of you." Before the wedding service at the *chuppah*, (a canopy under which a Jewish couple stand during their wedding ceremony), Charles took separate pictures with his family while I waited in the bridal room for my turn to be photographed with my family. After this, I went to the smorgasbord room where everybody was waiting for me to arrive. I never felt so special in my entire life. After I was diagnosed with bipolar disorder, I did not think anyone would marry me, but I was wrong. For that one day, I was happy to be the center of attention. I deserved it after struggling so hard to find the right person. The only thing I wished was for my mother to be with me, and she was, in a spiritual way.

While I was in the smorgasbord (party) room, Charles was with the men in the library, praying *mincha* (an afternoon prayer service) where they also said special prayers for our mothers who could not be at our wedding. Rabbi Algaze, along with Rabbi Solomon, the rabbi at *Seaview Jewish Center*, made sure the marriage certificate and *ketubah* (a Jewish document outlining the rights and responsibilities of the groom in relation to the bride) were signed so that the *ketubah* could be read at the service. At the signing, there is a religious custom for mothers to break the plate, but my cousin Sharon and Charles's sister did it instead.

At the party room, I waited till Charles came in with our fathers to cover my face with the veil that had been put on my head. While the men were singing and dancing, our fathers put their right hands on my head, as did Rabbi Algaze, and blessed me. I never felt so much joy in my life. This was a real recovery for me because it put an end to my single years. After having so much trouble revealing my mental illness to men who did not want me, and as I walked down the aisle with my father, I knew that Charles was the right man for me to spend the rest of my life with.

When I walked down the aisle with my father, I felt there was someone missing. It was my mother. I could not smile and looked down as if I was depressed until one of the seated guests cried out, "Smile!" and I did. Once I arrived at the *chuppah*, I had to walk around Charles seven times which is the custom for orthodox Jews. I only walked around four times because I got very nervous when my wedding gown got caught in the microphone wire. I felt so embarrassed, but can look back now and laugh at this.

After Rabbi Algaze recited the Hebrew marriage blessing for Charles and me, we both drank some wine. Then, Charles repeated the Hebrew blessing that Rabbi Algaze told him to say while he put the ring on my finger. Rabbi Solomon then read our *ketubah* for us and recited prayers of remembrance for our mothers which made Charles and I and our family very sad. After the seven blessings were recited and Rabbi Algaze made an official blessing in English, Charles stepped on the glass and broke it and everyone congratulated us on our marriage.

When the service was over, Charles and I went to a private room where we would be alone together. Then we joined everyone in the reception room with the singing and dancing. During the meal, my cousin Sharon gave a speech and wished both of us a great life together. Charles and I were finally husband and wife. We overcame so much in our lives to be able to reach this special moment and deep inside us, we both knew that our mothers were at our wedding in spirit. They will never be gone as long as they remain in our hearts forever.

CHAPTER 9

RECOVERY DURING MARRIAGE

When the wedding was over, Charles and I moved into our new apartment. That week, we were invited every night for seven meals (this is a Jewish custom known as *sheva brachos* (seven blessings), by some friends who could not be at our wedding and who wanted to celebrate with us as husband and wife. Once the *sheva brachos* were over, we went to Orlando, Florida for our honeymoon. We stayed at the *Radisson Hotel* where there was a kosher restaurant nearby for us. Charles and I also visited *Walt Disney World, Seaworld,* and *Epcott Center.* We had an amazing time, but some days were not so great. Once, at *Walt Disney World,* I made Charles go on the *Space Mountain,* a roller coaster ride in the dark where you could not see anything. I had been on this ride before when I was seven, but had forgotten how dangerous this ride could be. When we got off the *Space Mountain,* Charles was very sick and thought he was going to die, so he got very angry at me. His anger turned into rage and this was a side of him I had never seen before. This was the first time I realized how his mental illness could have an impact on me. When Charles got upset, I started to cry and wanted to give my wedding band back to him, but Charles started to calm down and apologized, which made the rest of the week fun and romantic for us again. I learned that when he has a rage and I start to cry so hard, we have no control over our depression. Because we are both emotional and love each other so much, we discussed why we were upset and tried to talk about the mistakes we made so that this would not happen again.

When our trip from Florida came to an end, Charles and I flew back home and started to concentrate on living our lives with each other. Charles went back to work at his job at *BSA Advertising* and I went back to *Transitional Services of New York* to look for a job in the mental health field. This was our way of starting as a couple in our recovery process from mental illness. We also continued treatment with our psychiatrists and therapists. Sometimes if an issue arose between Charles and me, he would meet with my therapist, Barbara Liss, who was a certified social worker and marriage counselor, so we could search for solutions to our problems as a married couple. Although Charles's therapist was in Manhattan at that time, I only went once or twice because of the long distance.

At *Transitional Services of New York*, I took a variety of workshops to help me find employment. I did not only look in the mental health area, but also at other nonprofit agencies, such as universities and Jewish organizations.

During that year, Charles and I looked for synagogues that we could join to become members and continue to support Judaism and Israel. After a long search, we finally decided to become members of the *Young Israel of Kew Gardens Hills*. It was a great community to be part of. When we became members of this temple, we noticed that the *Orthodox Union* was planning a one week trip to Israel. Since Charles and I had never been to Israel as a married couple, we decided to take this trip. It was a great feeling for us to put some distance between our families and work related problems and it felt refreshing to get away from our mental health issues. In a way, going to Israel was our own way of establishing recovery for ourselves.

We left for Israel in the middle of January 2004 as part of a group with the *Orthodox Union*. When we arrived, Charles and I stayed at the *Sheraton Hotel* in Jerusalem. Every day we would get breakfast but were on our own for the rest of the meals except for the Sabbath. On our first day in Israel, we took a tour of Jerusalem. Charles and I went first to Yad Vashem, the memorial for six million Jews who perished in the *Holocaust*. It showed us how our struggles with mental illness seemed to be almost insignificant compared to those Jews who lost their lives, which is why *Yad Vashem* was built. Then we took a tour through the *Old City* and went through the *Jewish Quarter* and visited the *Western Wall* (the Kotel). This too reminded us of our history as Jewish people and those who lost their lives to protect and defend Israel. I believe that our lives have been very blessed by God. Neither of us wanted to become mentally ill, but when we compare ourselves to those who died trying to defend our Holy Land, I feel that being able to live, even with a mental illness, is a blessing from God. It is a way of thinking that God developed some type of plan for Charles and me, even though we do not know where it may lead to.

After we finished our sightseeing, we went to visit my parents' relatives. It was the first time they met Charles. They liked him because of how cute he was and also because he had a sense of humor. We showed them our wedding pictures and spoke about how our families were holding up since our mothers had passed away. Then

Sabbath came and we went to the *Western Wall* with a group of people that Friday evening. We prayed and put little pieces of paper inside the corners of the wall which contained our wishes and hopes for the future. For Charles and me it was to have *parnossah* (Yiddish word for livelihood) and children. The meals we had were wonderful, and on Sabbath we prayed at the *Great Synagogue* opposite the hotel. When we were ready to leave, the group stopped at the *Western Wall* to pray one last time so that we would have a safe trip back home. Charles and I never wanted to leave Israel but had no choice since our families and work related duties were back in America. We also had to continue seeing our psychiatrists and therapists on a weekly basis because this was a top priority in order for us to stay well mentally and physically. Charles and I were happy that we made this trip but it was time for us to come home and get settled back into a life with hopes and dreams.

When we came home, Charles returned to his job at *BSA Advertising* and continued his mental health treatment with his psychiatrist and therapist. I also went back to the *Advanced Center for Psychotherapy* where I continued to see Dr. Blair Skolnick, my psychiatrist, and Barbara Liss, my therapist.

At this time, I decided to go back to my vocational program at *Transitional Services of New York*. I started to look for work in the mental health area again because I knew I would be happy and accepted there. It was a place where I could help other people get well and achieve recovery from mental illness in their own way and at their own speed.

My neighbor at the co-op apartment where I lived told me

that she worked for *PSCH*, a non-profit agency. *PSCH* stands for Promoting Specialized Care and Health. I knew that this organization helped individuals with both mental and developmental disabilities, so I gave her my resume to give to Human Resources. When she told me that *PSCH* was conducting interviews at an *Open House for Direct Care Counselors* to work with developmental disabilities, I went with the hope of being interviewed by someone from Human Resources in the mental health department. I filled out an application, brought my resume and my articles which were published in *New York City Voices*. As luck would have it, a woman from Human Resources interviewed me for a position as a peer counselor. When the interview was over, I thanked her and then a week later got a call from a woman named Shavone Hamilton. She was the team leader of *PSCH's* ACT team. *ACT* stands for Assertive Community Treatment. This program helps to reduce emergency room use and inpatient hospitalizations as well as providing individuals with personal needs relating to housing, medication management, substance abuse, socialization, and employment. *ACT* also helps those who live in homeless shelters to make the transition into community housing and provides support to help people live independently in the community.

The hours and days I had to work were very flexible. The only thing I did not like was going to the homeless shelters alone, so I asked Ms. Hamilton if it would be okay to go with a co-worker so that I would feel safe. She told me that it would be fine. Two days later, I received a call from Human Resources telling me that I got the job. It was such a surprise for me because I had no formal training as a peer counselor, but belonging to a vocational program at *Transitional Services of New York*, the articles I had published in *New*

York City Voices, and the fact that I was a recipient of mental health services, helped them make the decision to offer me the job.

I started working for *PSCH's ACT* team after Passover and traveled to their location in Jamaica, Queens by bus. On my first day, I learned all about my job and some of my duties which were to provide peer support to their clients, research other agencies where they could seek help, conduct groups on housing, vocations, and other issues. I also participated in the staff meetings as they read their progress notes about each client they visited the previous day. On the second day, the team leader showed me where all the clients' files were and taught me how to write service plans and progress notes for each of the clients. During the first two months, I had to attend *ACT* training seminars at a place called *Pathways to Housing* in Harlem. These seminars taught me what to expect when working for an *ACT team*, like the one at *PSCH*. It also showed me how to fill out the service plans and forms for Section 8 Housing. After the seminars were over, I received a certificate which let my employer know that I attended the program. Because my job title was Peer Counselor, *PSCH* also sent me to my first peer specialist conference. I met several people at the conference that I knew from previous vocational programs I had attended in the past. There was a variety of workshops and speakers who spoke about their experiences with mental illness and their recoveries. After these trainings were over, I learned little by little about the job. As a peer counselor, I helped four major staff workers. They were the housing specialist, vocational specialist, *MICA* specialist, and the nurse.

When I worked with the housing specialist, I went to a few homeless shelters where some of our people lived until they found housing through Section 8. Once they found housing, I often helped escort them to certain services they needed for moving into a new apartment. Some of these services were to help them maintain a budget to buy food, clothing, gas, electricity, furniture, and phone use. Once the housing specialist asked me to go to a certain client's apartment and wait for someone from the housing authority's Section 8 to check the condition of the client's apartment. I waited there for a long time. By the afternoon, the staff worker from Section 8 finally came and so did the housing specialist. All of us went inside the apartment together to make sure the client's apartment passed inspection. I also visited some individuals who were already living in their apartments to make sure there were no problems. If there were, I would write them down on the progress notes and discuss them with the rest of the staff, since we all worked as a team. I also took over some groups which the housing specialist wanted me to when she was out in the field. Because I did not know that much about housing, I often researched it on the internet. Mostly, I brought in topics on how to budget one's money by keeping a journal in order to pay for rent, food, clothing, etc. These are some areas where the housing specialist needed my assistance.

I helped the people, together with the vocational specialist, get back to work once they took care of their housing goals. They needed jobs to help them pay their rent, food, clothing, and other expenses. To get a job, I taught some of the people on a one to one basis how to write cover letters and resumes, and practice their interviewing skills through role play with some difficult questions. Some of their resumes were not professional so I looked on the internet for some sample resumes they could use. Once corrected on paper, I helped them make their resumes more outstanding. Because some of the individuals had gaps in their resumes, I suggested that they seek help from a vocational program or do some volunteer work. Some people did not even have a high school diploma so I found schools where they offered free classes to get their GED. Some people wanted to be peer counselors like me, so I suggested programs like *Howie the Harp Peer Advocacy Center* and *Goodwill Industries of N.Y. and N.J.*, where they offered training for this type of work.

I also conducted groups when the vocational specialist was out in the field. To help these people with their interviewing skills, I gave them a multiple choice practice test that showed which question had the best answer. At the group, we also discussed how to dress appropriately for an interview and maintain good posture and eye contact. Another example of what I did in the group was to conduct a test of their personality to see how it would fit to a particular job. If a person was introverted, they might not want a job where there were too many people around, and would want to find a job that could be done on a one-to-one basis. An example would be a home health aide position. Someone who was extroverted might want a job in sales or a career as a lawyer where one would deal with many people. As a result, helping the vocational specialist was the best part of my job because I have always had an interest in teaching others how to get and retain employment. Doing this would help me prepare for other jobs in the near future.

Due to the fact that I did not have enough knowledge on substance abuse issues, I was unable to help the *MICA* specialist. When I conducted groups with him, I decided to study the curriculum books they had on certain abusive drugs like cocaine, narcotics, and alcohol. I also volunteered to write different articles on the subject itself. As a peer counselor, I realized that some people might not only have a mental illness as a disease, but might also suffer from what they are addicted to as well. Since these addictions affect the mind, this can result in a relapse if treatment is not sought for both.

Helping the nurse was also interesting, especially when I went with him to meet his clients at their apartments or homeless shelters. I watched how he took their blood pressure, pulse, temperature, and also realized the importance of having them take their medications. He told me that as a peer counselor, you had to watch them count the number of pills they were supposed to take and check if any medications needed refills. I also learned that it was part of my job to remind the people of their next appointment with the psychiatrist and to come to group.

When the nurse was out in the field, I often conducted some of his groups, as I did with the rest of the staff. At the group, we discussed how important it was to continue treatment in order to avoid a relapse. We also talked about the different types of medications some of our people were taking and that if a problem arose they should speak to their psychiatrist.

Consequently, working as a peer counselor with the *ACT* team was my first real job as a mental health advocate. It made me see that some of these individuals went through greater hardships then I could ever imagine. I knew that this was the career I wanted because I liked helping people and noticed how passionate and motivated I could be in this field. I also thought doing work in this field would be a place where I could feel accepted and appreciated, because it became a place where I could continue to recover and fight for the mentally ill.

CHAPTER 10

STRUGGLING WITH INFERTILITY

After Charles and I came back from Israel in 2004, we talked about having a child and tried to go about it naturally. When we realized that I was not getting pregnant after six months, we saw a doctor who showed us through drawings how to have sexual intercourse, but we did not have success. While working for *PSCH*, Charles and I went to see my gynecologist who recommended a fertility specialist at *Cornell Medical Center*. His name was Dr. Steven Spandorfer. We met with the doctor who suggested we try intrauterine insemination.

For a few months we went through the process of taking my husband's sperm and putting it directly into my uterus, but as each month went by, I kept getting my period, which was a disappointment for the both of us. It was tough on me, getting up early in the morning and having to miss work on certain days. Although my supervisor was very understanding about the whole situation, I felt guilty. I knew that I had to resign from my job because going from doing inseminations and then going to work exhausted me. I also realized that I needed rest and relaxation if I was ever going to get pregnant. As a result, in March 2005 I gave notice and told my employer that I could not work and seek fertility help at the same time. *PSCH* gave me their blessing and I continued forward trying to get pregnant.

Getting pregnant was the major focal point in my life, and in a way, it became an obsession. According to Jewish law, having children was a necessity because I had been taught that the role of a Jewish woman was to procreate and bring forth children into the world so that the Jewish race could multiply, as our matriarchs (*Sarah, Rebecca, Rachel and Leah*) did. I went through six inseminations and each time got my menstrual period. Dr. Spandorfer did not want to give up on me. He wanted to check and see if my uterus was functioning properly by using a camera and inserting some kind of dye into my vagina. This was very painful because it gave me terrible cramps. As it turned out, everything was fine.

After this, my husband and I visited him in his office and he suggested we try fertility drugs. Dr. Spandorfer prescribed *Clomid* and told me to take it for about five days during my menstruation. Then he waited until the eggs in my ovaries grew into follicles. When they did, he saw three of them through the ultrasound. Once the follicles reached their maximum growth, Charles and I did another intrauterine insemination. Two weeks later, I got my period. The nurses advised me to come in after two weeks even if I got my period so they could do a pregnancy test, but I did not listen. I thought once my period came, there would be no sense to come in. I continued to take the *Clomid*. When my doctor came back from vacation, he advised me to come in and do an ultrasound. One Sunday, I tested myself and knew I was ovulating. I called the hospital and they said that Charles and I should come in to do another insemination. Before the insemination, Dr. Spandorfer wanted to check my ovaries by ultrasound again. He then noticed something was growing in my uterus. He thought I could be pregnant but that was too good to be true because I had just had my period. This was around June 2005. The doctor immediately took a blood test and checked my urine and found that the pregnancy hormone was positive and told me I was pregnant.

When I found out I was pregnant, I called my father and told him the news. He was filled with joy. I was never so happy and realized that I did not have to go for tests or fertility treatments any more. I therefore felt this pregnancy was a gift from God. I saw Dr. Spandorfer two more times. Through the ultrasound, I heard the heartbeat of the fetus and saw a picture of what was going to turn out to be our baby. However, little did I know that the next five months of my pregnancy would turn out to be tragic.

In the first two months of my pregnancy, the fetus was doing well. After I was finished with Dr. Spandorfer, I went back to Dr. Stephan Schuster, my gynecologist and obstetrician. It felt good to know that everything was all right with the fetus. I started to suffer from morning sickness, which was not easy to go through. At this time, I was still under psychiatric care and my psychiatrist did not want me to go off my medications because he thought I might slip into a relapse. Dr. Schuster sent my husband and me to a genetics counselor to check and see what effect the drugs I was taking would have on the fetus. Charles and I knew that the baby would have a fifteen percent chance of developing a mental illness as the baby got older. It is true that we had some concerns and were a little bit anxious about our child having a mental illness like us, but this was expected. With all the precautions, I went into a relapse which had nothing to do with the medications I was taking. It had to do with problems at home.

Everyone in the family was happy that I was pregnant, but my father who wanted nothing but the best for me, triggered one of the worst depressions that I had had in a along time. I was concerned about the pregnancy, but my father burdened me even more with his worries. My father meant well and had a good heart, but he could not stop himself from being overprotective of me.

Some of the issues that had set off my depression were that my father believed my husband and his family's genes had some birth defects which could affect the fetus growing inside me. Every time he reminded me of this, I held back the tears and began to lose my strength. My father also said that my husband's carpal tunnel syndrome was something he was born with and thought the fetus might develop this problem. Whether these things were true or not, I did not want to hear them. Since my sister-in-law did not have any children, my father assumed that she had a problem and not because her husband did not want children. This was not so, and even if it were, I accepted my husband and his family's problems whatever they were, once I got married. It was all fine with me, but my father did not see it that way. Every time he repeated these remarks, I was hurt, weak, and so depressed, that I could not stop crying. The nurses at Dr. Schuster's office warned me of how this depression would not be good for the pregnancy.

Near the end of September 2005, Dr. Schuster wanted me to have a sonogram that would test if there were any abnormalities with the fetus. When the results came back, they were positive.

There was an abnormality and it showed that the fetus might have *spinal bifida*. At this time, Dr. Schuster told me that I had to switch to another obstetrician. I was so frustrated about this because I was in the middle of my pregnancy. I finally switched to Dr. Raphael Reiss who I felt happened to be a very good obstetrician.

Before I met the doctor, my father insisted that the whole family come and discuss the abnormality of the pregnancy. It was like an intervention. I was already weak, tired, and depressed, and did not want to be burdened with any more worries until I saw the new doctor. My Aunt Bertha was there, so I came hoping she could talk some sense into my father by telling him this is not the way to treat a woman when she is pregnant, especially when that woman has a mental illness. However, she sided with my father. My father was not a patient person and started to interfere. He said that I must have an amniocentesis (a procedure that is used to detect genetic disorders such as *Down syndrome*), before I even met Dr. Reiss. This made my depression even worse. My hormones were so high that I left his home angry and upset because I could not handle the pressure. My husband saw how much I was suffering so he suggested I see my psychiatrist immediately. My psychiatrist did not want to prescribe any more medications because he thought the situation with my pregnancy could make it worse.

When I met Dr. Reiss, he advised me to see another genetics counselor and do the amniocentesis like my father wanted. Hearing it from the doctor and not from my father made me feel better about it. Although my father's interference was out of love for me, my father was not a professional and there was a big difference because the doctor was objective and not subjective like my father.

My husband and I met with the genetics counselor at *Long Island Jewish Hospital* and told her everything about our family's history and our diagnoses with mental illness. She explained the process of the amniocentesis and what it would show and scheduled an appointment to have it done that very same day. I was scared and nervous because of the needle they would put directly into my abdomen. I was glad that Charles was with me because I needed to hold him since the pain was so unbearable. During the procedure, I heard one of the nurses say that there was bleeding inside the abdomen. I was so worried that something was wrong, not just with the fetus, but also with me.

After the results came in and another ultrasound was done, Dr. Reiss told me the fetus was not growing because of the loss of amniotic fluid and lack of nutrition from the placenta. Dr. Reiss sent me to Dr. Fleischer, an obstetrician at *Long Island Jewish Hospital*, for a consultation. Dr. Fleischer specialized in high risk pregnancies and we consulted with him to see if anything could be done so that the fetus could survive. This time, I wanted my father and husband to be there because I was very depressed and scared and did not want to go through this alone. Dr. Fleischer did another ultrasound and told us that if I decided to keep the baby it would be born prematurely and might have severe complications because the organs were not fully developed. He also said that there was a possibility that the baby could be stillborn. I realized the severity of the situation and became more depressed and scared not only for the baby, but also for myself. Dr. Fleischer recommended that I terminate the pregnancy or wait until I miscarried on my own. I did not want to wait because the bleeding from the miscarriage would be too painful. Since there was no chance of the fetus surviving, I knew I had to terminate the pregnancy and because the procedure would be done in the hospital, I knew I would not feel any pain.

While I was getting ready to terminate the pregnancy, I wondered if the stress and depression that my father caused me at the beginning of the pregnancy had anything to do with the fetus not being able to survive. Even though the doctors said this was not true, I still could not stop thinking about it. A day before the procedure, my father picked me up from the hospital and I spoke to him about an article I had read that stated how having too much stress and depression could make things worse with a baby's health during pregnancy. My father got very excited and again mentioned the problems with my husband's and his family's genes. I was so hurt and angry that I had a fight with him in the car and told him that I did not want him at the hospital while the procedure was being done. As soon as I arrived home, I was so depressed that I cried my heart out and had to call my husband at work so he could be with me during the procedure instead of my father.

Until this day, I have not gotten over the pregnancy and will always have doubts and never know the real reason why the fetus could not survive. When I brought up the subject to my father, he got very angry and did not recall the depression he brought on during those early months of my pregnancy. Like most parents, he cannot understand the meaning of mental illness. When a woman is pregnant and has a mental illness, one should not cause more depression during this time in her life.

Sometimes I wonder if having had a miscarriage would have been better for me than choosing to terminate the pregnancy. At least if I had had a miscarriage, it would have been God's decision to end the pregnancy, and not mine. I often think that maybe he was punishing me for something I had done in the past. Either way, whether it would have been the miscarriage or the decision to terminate, God did not want me to have this baby. It made me realize that perhaps I was not capable or ready to raise a child at this point in my life.

A few months after the pregnancy was over, Dr. Reiss, my gynecologist/obstetrician, wanted me to see a hematologist at *Long Island Jewish Hospital* because he suspected from the results of a blood test that I might be at risk in developing blood clots. The hematologist did some more tests and found out that when I was pregnant, the placenta probably had some blood clots which blocked the fetus from getting the nutrition it was supposed to receive. The hematologist told me that if I chose to get pregnant again, I would have to take *Heparin*, a blood thinner that would prevent the clots from forming in the placenta and the fetus.

Despite the fact that I would have to take *Heparin*, my husband and I met with Dr. Spandorfer, our fertility specialist, and we decided to try to conceive again. I have to admit that because of the struggles and pains I went through in the first pregnancy, and the fact that I would be at such a high risk for the next pregnancy, part of me was nervous to go through the process again. However, I did not care because I wanted a child.

Dr. Spandorfer wanted me to take *Clomid* again through insemination, since that is what got me pregnant the first time. The doctor used *Clomid* for three intrauterine inseminations, but it failed to get me pregnant. After that, the doctor used a fertility drug called *Gonal-f* whereby I had to give myself shots, but I was still unable to get pregnant. At this point, I was getting tired of going from one treatment to another. The treatments not only affected me physically, but also mentally. Waking up early every morning to go to Manhattan where the *Center for Reproductive Medicine* at *Cornell Medical Center* was located, and coming home exhausted, wore me out emotionally. Dr. Spandorfer wanted me to try Invitro Fertilization (*IVF*), but Charles and I learned how expensive it was. We went to a class at the hospital that explained the whole process of Invitro Fertilization. It was so overwhelming for Charles and me that we took a rest from continuing with the treatments.

When we asked *Bonei Olam*, a funding organization that would help pay for the *IVF*, they rejected us the first time. Since we did not have the insurance or the money to pay for the *IVF*, Charles and I told Dr. Spandorfer that we had had enough and wanted to seek help from other fertility specialists that might be able to help us with what we could afford.

One morning, I woke up and started to cry and became very emotional about the treatments. Going from one fertility specialist to another caused my mental health to suffer. My husband and I had had enough and decided to stop for a while. We thought of adoption, but my father interfered and did not want us to adopt. Then Charles and I began to think that living without children might be the best thing for us. In the beginning, the thought of living child-free made us feel sad because we both knew that if we chose this route, we would never become parents. However, there were also advantages, such as going back to school for a new career, not having to discipline a child, and the freedom to go out and travel.

At this time, I decided that I wanted to go back to school and get my Masters in Social Work. Since I could not have children, I wanted to have a career. Charles and I made an appointment with my father's colleague, Dr. Bernard Lander, founder of Touro College. He tried to help Charles get a job at Touro and helped me get accepted into their social work program. I then met with Dr. Steven Huberman, *Dean of the Social Work Program*, and saw how intrigued he was about my experiences as a peer counselor and my recovery from mental illness. He suggested that I take one course and see how I would do, and decide whether or not social work was the right field for me. This felt like I was being put on probation instead of being accepted into the program. Dr. Huberman met with my husband Charles to also see if he could get him a job at Touro College.

The course was difficult and in a way helped me try to overcome the idea of not having children. While I was taking the course, I wanted to get a job in human services. There was only one place I knew that had such a program and it was called *Howie the Harp Peer Advocacy and Training Center*. This center trains people with mental illness in how to become peer specialists and then helps them seek employment. Since I had the experience, I applied to their *Assisted Competitive Employment* and got accepted.

I thought going to school and looking for a job would help me get over my problem of not having children, but it did not. Every time I went to temple, I would either see babies with their mothers or women who were pregnant. This upset me because I had stopped trying. School and work did not seem as important to me as having a child, so I convinced my husband and father to let me try again for what would be the last time. Once my course was finished, I decided to leave the social work program and concentrate on looking for a job and go back for my fertility treatments.

During the time I was at *Howie the Harp*, I attended their program which included going to a job support group called *Career Club*. They sent out my resume and I had several job interviews, one of which landed me a job as a peer specialist with an agency called *ACMH*, the Association for Rehabilitative Case Management and Housing. *ACMH* is a housing program in which people live in scattered site apartments. I decided to take the position while looking for a fertility specialist. One of my friends recommended this special Chinese physician named Dr. Zhang. He ran his own fertility clinic and his methods were different from most traditional physicians such as Dr. Spandorfer from *Cornell*. Dr. Zhang treated women who were over thirty-seven years old and into their early forties. He did not give many fertility drugs which could produce ten to twelve eggs because he knew most women that age could only develop three to five eggs.

Throughout all this, I realized how tired I was. I also knew I was unable to keep my job at *ACMH* because it was too stressful to work and go for the treatments, so I left. *Howie the Harp* was disappointed because I had gotten the job through them. I concentrated on my fertility treatments with Dr. Zhang who did two *IVF* procedures, but both were unsuccessful. He kept encouraging me to try and try again but I could not afford it. I went back to *Bonei Olam*, the agency that helped women with the cost of the treatments. After going through several months of treatments, *Bonei Olam* was not willing to pay Dr. Zhang any more money because each treatment

I had was unsuccessful. *Bonei Olam* suggested that I see another fertility specialist, Dr. Licciardi at *N.Y.U. Medical Center*. I went for a consultation with my father to learn why I was not getting pregnant. Dr. Licciardi reviewed my records and told me that I was not responding to the fertility drugs and suggested I try egg donation or adoption. Dr. Licciardi and his staff gave me a blood test and suggested I give *IVF* one more try. *Bonei Olam* agreed to pay the rest after I paid the first five thousand dollars. Every few days they examined me and noticed that I only produced two follicles with the fertility drugs they had prescribed for me. Dr. Licciardi cancelled the *IVF* cycle and did an insemination instead, but that too was unsuccessful.

After that, Charles and I agreed that this would be the last one because we were both emotionally exhausted and could not handle the stress which was bad for my mental health. We knew we had to move on with our lives but I was still very depressed when the doctors told me that I was unable to get pregnant again.

A few months later, my husband and I talked about adoption since it was the only way we could have a child of our own. We went to one adoption agency and filled out the application. However, there was one question they asked that felt too personal and discriminating which was, "Have you ever had a mental illness?" I thought this was unfair considering what my family and I had been through. My best friend reminded me how hard it would be for us to raise a child not only because of our mental health, but also because of our family problems. When I told my father what she had said, he told me that she was right. I cried so hard because people still noticed how weak I could be in certain situations. I was upset and angry with my friend, but in the long run I knew she was right. My friend gave me another option and that was to try foster care adoption. If I could not handle a particular child, I could give it back to the agency. My husband and I went through *Ohel Children's Home and Family Services*. This was a Jewish agency which provided assistance to Jewish children who had developmental and psychiatric disabilities. They also had a foster care adoption program which Charles and I applied to and started taking parenting classes in. *Ohel* took their time and it was hard to get in touch with them. Then one day, I came to the realization that perhaps living without children was the best thing for us. It was hard for me to even think about it, so I decided to read books and pamphlets about childfree living because this was going to change my life forever.

Reading these books showed me the advantages of a life without children. I could concentrate on a career, build an intimate relationship with my husband Charles, and also travel whenever or wherever I chose to go. One of the books, *Sweet Grapes*, also taught me how to heal and say goodbye to never being able to have children. It also taught me not to use the term, "childless," and to be content with whatever made me happy in life. This book also showed me that I can still love and see other people's children and not feel sad or depressed because I didn't have what others had. There are so many ways to have children in your life such as volunteering as a Big Sister, tutoring, helping with homework, and being an aunt-like figure. For example, every Sabbath afternoon I would visit my friend's children and read them books and play with them. This made me happy and gave me a good feeling knowing that I was loved by them, even though these children were not mine. I also saw how hard it could be to raise a child and maintain order and discipline, which are things I do not know how to do and therefore am glad that Charles and I do not have to cope with these responsibilities, which may seem selfish. In actuality and throughout my life, I have always had problems relating to children. Another reason is our mental illness. I know deep down that with me having bipolar disorder and with Charles having depression, we would not be able to deal with the overwhelming stress of taking care of a child's needs and wants.

Living childfree has made me feel happy again and I strongly believe that if God wanted me to have children, I would have had them. It has also made me realize that having a mental illness was God's decision, which made me think that this was the life he wanted for me in order to face other challenges that would test my mental health yet again.

CHAPTER 11

WORKING WHILE MY FATHER WAS SICK

Knowing now my decision to live a childfree life was an acceptable one, I decided to take a look at the advantages that my future might bring. The first thing I wanted was to start working again in the mental health field. Due to the fact that I had been away from the working world, I decided to volunteer with an organization that helped people with mental illness to become educated and find jobs. The organization that I chose to volunteer for was Federation Employment and Guidance Services known as *FEGS*. I volunteered as a peer counselor where I ran groups for issues such as assertiveness training, writing workshops, interviewing skills through role play, and symptom management. To get information on these topics, *FEGS* had binders for each topic that I would use for some of my groups. At that time, *FEGS* had a program called *IPRT* (Intensive Psychiatric Rehabilitation Treatment). In February, *FEGS* changed from *IPRT* to *PROS* (Personalized Recovery Oriented Services). When *FEGS* started using *PROS*, it became very hectic in the beginning, not just for the participants, but also for the staff. We had to learn a whole new curriculum and teach our participants new topics like *WRAP* (Wellness Recovery Action Plan). This is a plan that taught the participants how to recover by staying in treatment. Another new topic was teaching our participants how to live a healthy lifestyle by getting good nutrition and sleeping well at night.

While volunteering at *FEGS*, I noticed that my father was not well and had to have two cataracts removed. My father's legs were also starting to get weak which made it difficult for him to walk, and therefore, he needed a cane to balance himself. Around May, I decided to leave *FEGS* because my father had to undergo a heart procedure and had to have two stents placed in two of the arteries in his heart. He had the procedure and it was a success.

After my father's heart procedure, he had to take certain medications. One of them was *Plavix*, a blood thinner that was used to prevent any more clots in his heart. While my father recuperated at home, I started to go on job interviews and went back to *Transitional Services of New York* to get support from them in helping me land a job. As it turned out, I did not need much help. One of the places where I interviewed was at *Howie the Harp Peer Advocacy Center*, a place where they train people with mental illness to become peer specialists. This was part of an organization called *Community Access*.

Community Access is a place where they help people with psychiatric disabilities not only to find work, but also housing. I had three interviews with them. The first one was with *Howie the Harp*, where I met the director of the program, Mr. Dwayne Mayes. He was so popular around the mental health community that meeting him face to face was an honor for me. I was interviewed for over an hour and noticed how much he and the deputy director really liked me. After the first interview was over, I had a second interview with *Howie the Harp*. This time about twenty people interviewed me. This was something I never expected since it was the first time I was ever on a panel interview. I was so nervous, but the deputy director said I did fine. I waited another two weeks and then received a call from Mr. Mayes to go for a third interview with *Community Access*. Five people interviewed me and I could tell how impressed they were with the knowledge I had in the mental health community. After the last interview and a week later, Mr. Mayes offered me the job.

I started working for *Howie the Harp* in the beginning of August as an employment specialist. They trained me to run groups like the *Career Club* and the *Internship Support Group*. I also learned how to write progress notes for each client I met or spoke to on the phone. Even when I could not reach them by phone, I still had to write a progress note so Community Access would know that at least I had made an attempt to contact them. Eventually, I also received a caseload of my own clients. This made me feel important because I was put in charge of helping them get a job or an internship. Some clients were very aggressive and some missed their appointments with me to discuss their internship. This became too difficult to handle because I had trouble being assertive with them. I also attended staff meetings with the placement team which included my supervisor and two other employment specialists. At these meetings, I would share any problems I had with the clients who were assigned to me. As a result, I received good training and gained knowledge. I owed a lot to my supervisor, Gloria Goodson, and Mr. Mayes for helping me keep the job as long as I was able to.

While working, Mr. Mayes allowed me to go to Israel for the Jewish holidays, so Charles and I went and spent the holidays in Jerusalem. We went to the Western Wall and saw how crowded it was during *Succoth* and *Simchat Torah* (Jewish holidays). At the wall,

I prayed that my father would get better. After Israel, I went back to work for *Howie the Harp*. When I got back, my father's health got much worse. He had hemorrhoids and began to complain that they were painful, especially in the morning. My cousin Sharon, who was not working, took care of my father who was teaching her how to pay the bills and how to deal with businesses with which my father had difficulty. I tried to go and see him at least twice a week and go over investments that he had made for me. At this time, my father's stomach was getting bigger. He had developed something called *Ascites*, fluid in the abdomen, which was due to problems with his liver. When I called him from work, he had difficulty speaking to me and sometimes could not talk at all. When he spoke, I noticed how difficult it was for him to breathe. It was then that I realized my father was not going to survive another year.

Due to the fact that my father had a caretaker, I was able to continue working at *Howie the Harp*. I knew there would come a day when I would have to resign from my job as employment specialist. Eventually, I decided to tell *Community Access/Howie the Harp* about my father's illness and that I would have to be there in the event an emergency developed with my father. I felt it was my duty to prepare Mr. Mayes and my supervisor, Ms. Goodson, for the worsening situation with my father.

During this time, my father knew he was deteriorating and often said things like, "I want to die in my own bed at home." Every time he would talk like that I did not answer him, but kept silent. On the other hand, my cousin Sharon wanted to keep my father's spirits up and kept telling him that he had a lot to live for and that it was important for him to remain positive. However, I knew that she was not being realistic about his condition.

There were times when I wanted to see my father as often as I could, but because of work, I was only able to visit him twice a week. Any time I would tell my cousin Sharon that I was going to visit him, she gave me a hard time and would often tell me when to come or not to come. I did not appreciate this because I had a right to see him whenever I wanted, whether it was in the morning or in the afternoon. I realized that my cousin was only looking after my father's best interests, but I was his daughter and I also cared about him. When I talked to my father about this, he said I could come to visit him whenever I chose to because he knew I was working and did not have much free time. At times, when my father tried to explain things to me in private, especially financial matters, he had confidence in me and knew that I could grasp these things because I had majored in business when I had gone to college.

Sometimes, I felt jealous of my cousin because she had more time to take care of my father than I did, but I now realize how much my father needed her and that she was a great caregiver for him. Because of my mental illness, I do not think I would have done a better job taking care of my father than Sharon had done, but as long as I knew there were things such as financial matters that he depended on me for, I was happy.

Sometime in March, I got together with Charles's family and we discussed our plans for Passover. We decided to go to Kutchers Resort in the Catskills. Although my mind was all set to go, my heart kept telling me not to because this could be the last Passover I would ever spend with my father. I had doubts about leaving my father home alone for Passover, but I did not want to disappoint Charles or his family, since going away had been my idea. When I talked to my father about going to Kutchers with Charles's family, he encouraged me to do so because he felt it would be a lot more work for me if I stayed and celebrated the holiday at his house. My father said that as long as his caretaker was staying with him, it would be all right. Finally, I decided to go away even though throughout the whole trip my heart and mind were with my father. Passover at Kutchers was great except for my not getting along with Charles's brother-in-law. When the time came for us to leave, I was never so happy because I missed my father and wondered how he was getting along. I kept praying that my father would stay alive until I returned home. As it turned out, my prayers were answered.

When I came back, I told my father about the good times and the bad times I had at Kutchers with Charles's family. I also told my father that if I went away for a Jewish holiday again, it would be just with my husband. I also went back to work at *Howie the Harp* and was given more responsibilities going on site visits and visiting the clients at their work site.

My father's stomach and hemorrhoids were getting worse and his physician recommended that he have a procedure called *TIPS*, Transjugular Intrahepatic Portosystemic Shunt, whereby the surgeon would put a shunt (a tube) in the area that the fluid was leaking from. We did not know when this procedure was going to take place so I told my supervisor, Ms. Goodson, that I would have to take off from work on that day to be with my father.

After the Memorial Day weekend, my father was taken to the

emergency room at the hospital. All day at work, I knew something was wrong because there was no one at home when I called and guessed that my father had been taken to the hospital. It was then that I knew I had to quit my job because my father was getting much worse. The *TIPS* procedure was done on a Thursday, but a day before that, the doctor removed eleven liters of fluid from his stomach. While I sat in the waiting room, the doctor came in and told me that the procedure was a success.

I hoped that everything would be all right after that, but that was not the case. My father's physician, Dr. Feinerman, came and told my father that his ammonia levels were very high and that they had to give him special medications for this. For a while, my father could not eat or drink anything because he was so weak from the procedure.

Throughout this period, I continued my treatment with my psychiatrist and therapist which was very helpful to me. Because I was dealing with a lot of stress and anxiety, Dr. Khaimov, my psychiatrist at that time, prescribed another medication called *Zanax* to reduce my anxiety and to help me relax. At times, this medication made me sleepy. My therapist, Bernice Talmatch, also helped me to prepare for what would happen in the event my father would die. She even arranged to have a session with my cousin Sharon and me so that we would be prepared in my father's time of need. However, my cousin disagreed with my therapist on so many issues and did not want to see her again. Therefore, my therapist had to teach me ways of dealing with my cousin's behavior so that I would not make the situation worse when my father was sick and in the hospital.

A few days after my father had the procedure, he started to eat again and regain his strength while at the hospital. My father was unable to walk and his doctor and social worker advised him to go for rehabilitation at a nursing home. My father never wanted to set foot in a nursing home and sometimes I think I should have taken him home to rehabilitate, but I followed the doctor's advice and sent him to *Meadow Park Rehabilitation Center* in Fresh Meadows, Queens. It was then that I gave my two weeks' notice at work and made the decision to quit my job. While I was finishing up at work, I visited my father at *Meadow Park*. The place was not that great. Twice my father had to change rooms until he finally got a room of his own. I thought he was getting better but by the end of the week he developed pneumonia and was sent back to the emergency room at the hospital.

During my last week at work, I left early every day to visit my father at the hospital. Due to the pneumonia, my father was in a coma for five days. Each day I prayed for him to wake up and whispered in his ear, "Please dad, do not give up this way." On my last day at work, I called the hospital to check and see if my father had opened up his eyes yet, and was told by the nurses that he had. After work, I went to the hospital and when I arrived there, my father kept saying to me, "Take me home! Let me die in my own bed!" My heart was breaking, every bone in my body was aching, and tears welled up inside me waiting to spill out. One of the physicians came in to look at and talk to my father, asking him questions about what he remembered, telling him that the pneumonia could kill him if he was sent home now. My father said, "I don't care, it's my life!" It was hard for me to leave him alone like this, but eventually I had to go home, so I left without saying goodbye.

The next morning, I was on my way to the hospital when my cousin Sharon called to tell me that the nurses had put gloves on my father's hands to restrain him. She told me to be prepared in the event he tried to get me to take them off. When I arrived I saw my father with the gloves on tied to the rails of the bed. My father kept saying to me over and over "Have *rachmanot* (Hebrew word for pity) on me." In other words, he was begging me to take off the gloves. I felt like I wanted to give in to him, but I could not. Although it was so hard to say "No, I can't dad," I had to, or else without those gloves on, he would have removed the tube that had been inserted in his nose. This is the reason why the nurses had put gloves on him in the first place.

That very next day, which was Friday, June 24, 2011, I went to my father's room in the morning and was stunned to see an oxygen mask on his face. After seeing this, I could not control myself any longer. I started to cry in front of the social worker because I knew then that my father was deteriorating rapidly. Before I went back to see him, I quickly dried up my tears so that my father would not see me like this. I had to be brave and reassure my father that I would not let the physicians at the hospital put him on a respirator, since this was what was indicated on his health care proxy.

On Saturday, June 25, 2011, I went to services at my synagogue early in the morning and afterwards walked to the hospital and noticed my father's breathing was getting worse. I stayed with him until his caretaker came to relieve me so that I could go home and get some rest. While I was taking my nap, the caretaker called and said that my father's blood pressure was going down rapidly. I told her that I would come as quickly as possible. It was then that I knew he was dying. At around that time, I called my father's sister, Aunt Bertha, and told her the bad news and she cried while we were on the phone. She wanted to see him, but I told her it would not be a good idea since she herself was also not well. I really had not wanted to call her, but had felt she should know.

Later, my husband Charles came in and stayed with us until visiting hours were over. My father was breathing at a very fast pace. When we were on our way home, we received a call from one of the nurses telling us to come back and stay with him. The physician did not think he would survive the night. We went back and I called the rabbi of my synagogue to come and meet us at the hospital. I was prepared for everything so I brought along a black binder which my father had saved, containing all the information on what to do when he passed on. We met with Rabbi Yoel Schonfeld at the hospital who had stayed with us for a few hours and who told me who to contact when my father died. One of the physicians came to us and said that there was fluid in his lungs and that they wanted to do a procedure that would help him breathe easier. This was not a cure and it would not change his prognosis, so we finally made a decision and told the doctor to go ahead with the procedure. It was around midnight when the procedure was done.

Charles and I stayed throughout the night until morning. We went home to get some rest and came back to the hospital that Sunday afternoon. Some of our friends came to visit us and brought food so we would not be hungry. We could not stay in the hospital another night so we told the nurses to call us in case he passed away in his sleep. I could not sleep at night and had to take the *Zanax* medication my psychiatrist had prescribed to relieve some of the anxiety I felt. I did not receive any phone calls during the night, which meant that my father survived another night. At 7:00 in the morning, the nurses called and told us to come immediately, saying that our father might die at any moment. I arrived at the hospital at 8:15 a.m. and noticed that my father had a small movement on his neck, and on that Monday, June 27, 2011 at 9:25 a.m., he died. At that moment, I became very anxious and concentrated so hard on what to do next, that I could not calm down. Before I left the room, I wiped my tears, kissed him, and said my goodbyes to him.

CHAPTER 12

COPING WITH THE LOSS OF MY FATHER

After I left the hospital, I went to *Schwartz Brothers Funeral Home* in Forest Hills, Queens so I could make arrangements for my father's funeral which was to take place on the next day. I met with Ms. Jennifer Martin, the director, who discussed the costs and helped me select a casket. The casket I chose was made out of wood and had a nice design, and I thought that my father would be comfortable resting in it. When I was finished, I went home so that Charles and I could pack some clothes and stay at my parents' apartment. Charles and I stopped at our synagogue and met with Rabbi Yoel Schonfeld, our rabbi, and cried to him and his secretary about the death of my father. It was a very emotional time for me. My mind was all over the place and it almost felt as though my depression was coming back. When we arrived at my parents' home, I called our relatives and friends and told them when and where the funeral was going to be. I also gave them the address of where I was going to sit *shiva* so they could pay their respects.

The funeral was held the following day. I met with Ms. Martin and Rabbi Schonfeld who gave me instructions and tore off a piece of the shirt I was wearing. I also met with my father's sister, Aunt Bertha. Before the people began to arrive at the funeral home,

Ms. Martin let me identify the body and say goodbye to my father one last time. Since not many of my father's friends and relatives came, and because the service was held on a Tuesday when people were working, there was only a small crowd there. Rabbi Schonfeld talked about my father and described what a great man he was. He talked about his life both in Iraq and Israel, and how he came to the United States and became an educational director at conservative afternoon Hebrew schools. I gave a small eulogy about how my father taught me to be good to myself and to follow the teachings he taught me throughout my whole life. An example I cited was of the Jewish education he had provided for me. Rabbi Fabian Schonfeld recited the *kaddish* (a memorial prayer that is said for the dead), for all those who attended the funeral.

After the funeral, my husband, his family and I took the limousine that was waiting for us to go to *Beth Moses Cemetery* in Farmingdale, New York to bury my father next to my mother. It was very hard for me at the burial, but my cousin Sharon comforted me because I was crying so much. Rabbi Yoel Schonfeld said a few prayers and I shoveled some ground to cover my father's casket. When the burial was over, I went back to my father's apartment to start sitting *shiva*. When someone sits *shiva*, they have to wear the same clothes worn at the funeral and cannot bathe throughout the seven days of *shiva*. This is a Jewish custom which I observed out of respect for my father.

The *shiva* period was not an easy one for me because I was not getting along with my cousin Sharon. In fact, it was like a nightmare. Every time my friends would come over, she would interrupt us while talking, and therefore I could not speak freely about the relationship I had with my father. This upset me and I started to cry very hard in the other room and could not stop. When I would get on the phone with one of my friends and cry to them, my cousin would pick up an extension phone and interrupt my conversations. Even my husband Charles could not stand our quarrels and also had to watch what he said in front of my cousin. He missed my father so much that he also went into the room and cried his heart out. It was so hard for us because my cousin would not leave us alone for one minute and I felt this was unfair to Charles and me. I wanted my former psychiatrist to come and pay his respects but he told me over the phone that because my cousin was so intrusive, he felt it was best not to come and get involved. I never had such a miserable time. What I needed was peace and quiet, but that did not seem possible.

Yumi Ikuta, the deputy director at my former job at *Howie the Harp* came to visit me while I was sitting *shiva*. We talked about my father, our mental illness, and the changes that were going on at *Howie the Harp*. I also discussed with her and some members of my synagogue who were there about an event I had organized for the congregation on mental health. I told them that the speaker had been a social worker named Rosalie Wiener and about forty people had attended. Ms. Wiener had spoken about the major types of mental illnesses. After she had spoken, I had talked about how I coped with mental illness and my process of recovery. Having talked to the deputy director about this made me feel free for the first time. My cousin Sharon was busy talking to her friends and was not bothering me. When my friend Jordana came over, it felt so good to see her. I showed her pictures of some of the guests that were invited to my wedding. It also felt good because she was so supportive, but I was sad when she could not stay any longer.

After everyone left, my cousin was concerned about my having told people who came to visit me about my mental illness. She was especially upset when I discussed this while Yumi and Jordana were there. My cousin followed me into the other room and would not leave me alone. I lay down on the bed and could not stop crying because I felt so hurt. I did not think there was anything wrong in talking to Yumi and Jordana about my mental health. In all fairness, my cousin Sharon was worried on how this would have an impact on herself and her friends. She did not want any of her friends to know that I had a mental illness when we were sitting shiva for my father. She made me feel so ashamed for talking about it with my friends as if I had done something bad. I called my supervisor, Gloria Goodson, to talk about the incident that had just happened. My cousin interrupted my conversation with her which upset me even more, so I cried aloud and said, "Where are you daddy? I need you!" Charles came over and calmed me down and warned me not to discuss mental illness around my cousin because she was very sensitive to this subject and lacked education in the topic of mental health.

After this, I could not stay in my parents' home anymore so I left that Sunday night and finished sitting *shiva* at my place. It was such a relief to be at home with Charles again. When I came home, I called the friends who had been interrupted by my cousin when talking to me to see if this had made them feel uncomfortable. They all said that I did not need to apologize and that I had done nothing wrong.

That week, I was so upset that I called another cousin a couple of times. When he called back he said he was furious with me for calling and bothering him so many times. He told me if I did this again, he would not be my executor anymore. I was crying so much that the next morning I felt like I needed to go to the hospital. Charles took off from work and called my psychiatrist, Dr. Khaimov, who recommended I go to the psychiatric department at *Jamaica Hospital*. Charles called my cousin to come and drive us to the hospital. I told the doctor everything that had happened concerning my father's death and when I was sitting *shiva*. The doctor prescribed *Zanax* and gave me a higher dosage which made me sleepy. He did not see any reason to admit me, so we left. That afternoon I went to see my therapist with Charles. I told my therapist everything that had happened and she told me that an open expression of feeling is appropriate while sitting *shiva*. She also said that it is important for me to feel free to express myself without feeling edited. My therapist said that I had to respect my cousin's feelings, even if I felt she was wrong. In other words, my cousin Sharon may have had a point when I talked too much about mental illness to people outside the family. Even though I did this to try to educate others, she felt it was not appropriate at the time of *shiva*, which should have been spent talking about my father. As a result, I decided to see my therapist every week so that I could handle my cousin and see her in a different light and also because I missed my father very much.

Every morning when I woke up, I felt an emptiness that I had never felt before. I took the loss of my father very hard. I felt as if there was a hole in my heart that was ripped up to pieces. It was hard for me to feel anything else. When I laughed at something, I would quickly stop, not being sure if I had the right to ever feel happiness again. My husband Charles was very supportive and comforted me during this period in time.

One day, I decided to dispose of my father's clothes. I had an ache in my heart doing this. I could still smell his scent on his undershirts, and some of his shirts still looked brand new. I felt it was a shame to get rid of them, but I had to because there was no one I knew that was his size to give them to. Charles could not wear them because he was a lot heavier than my father. I also got rid of his shoes which smelled as if they were new and as though he had never worn them. It was not an easy task, but I managed.

On the 30th day after my father's funeral, and as is the Jewish custom during this period known as the *sheloshim* (a 30-day mourning period for immediate family), we went to the cemetery to visit his grave, as well as my mother's grave. In the evening, we had a gathering at the house so that those relatives who could not make it to the funeral and the *shiva* could offer their condolences. Most people who came were from my father's side of the family and we served food and beverages. Since my father was from Iraq, the men prayed in Sephardic melodies. (The Sephardic culture stems from certain European and Middle Eastern countries.) This was the last day for people to pay their respects to us. According to Jewish tradition, I had to mourn for one year. We said *kaddish* (a memorial prayer when one loses a very close relative), although according to Jewish tradition, women do not have to recite this prayer. However, I felt that I wanted to, so I said it at least twice a day. When I pray, I feel some spiritual uplifting which makes me feel that my father will always be with me.

After the thirty days were over, I wanted to get back to the life I had before my father had died and decided to do some volunteer work. Due to all the responsibilities I had with my father's estate,

I could not commit myself to take a job for a salary. I had hoped to be able to return to that some day and decided to stay in the mental health field and volunteer either at *Hands Across Long Island* or *Transitional Services of New York*. They are both non-profit organizations helping people recover from mental illness. They offer groups to its participants and talk with others who are faced with similar situations. When the participants are ready, they can start to look for employment.

I realize that I have to try my best to be patient and to get along with my cousin Sharon who has helped me throughout this process. She was the one who looked after my father when he was alive and I now realize I cannot forget that and therefore have to start to appreciate her. After all, she is a very close cousin to me and I love her dearly and need to understand her better.

In trying to deal with my losses, seeing my psychiatrist and therapist was not enough for me, so I decided to explore a bereavement group. There was a group in Long Island City called *Hospice of New York* which met the second and fourth Tuesday of every month. It helped me deal with my feelings in that there were others there who had also lost a parent. It was nice to share my story with them, and I could tell by their own stories just how much of a loss they suffered. I realized that this year was going to be a difficult one because I needed to focus on my father's estate. I also knew that it would take me a long time to get over his death.

I will probably have more conflicts with people as I go through the rest of the year in dealing with the loss of my father. However, I have learned one thing and that is that there is hope for me to get along with others, even if I sometimes have a quarrel with someone. I will always carry that thought with me because it was what my father had wanted for me. If there is one thing that I realize, it is that a parent never really dies as long as they remain in your heart.

CHAPTER 13
CONCLUSION

A s you have read, you can see that my mental health has been tested over and over during my recovery from mental illness. I have described to you most of the struggles that I have faced regarding mental illness. I know that there will be more challenges in the future which I must learn to overcome. Recovery is a long process and a person's recovery is different for everyone. So, if you have a mental illness, I will ask you, "What does recovery mean to you?" Better yet, what is the definition of recovery; what does it actually mean?

I think recovery literally means to get back into life. For example, recovery from a heart attack means changing your diet, taking medications prescribed by a doctor, exercise, and going for a stress test once a year. For people with mental illness, recovery does not just mean taking medications prescribed by a psychiatrist or talking about your problems to a therapist. It means getting back to what the human mind wants you to do. For example, getting back to work or school, exercising to reduce stress, having a balanced diet, meeting new people, going to a support group, and becoming a member of an organization like *NAMI* (National Alliance for the Mentally Ill) that helps fight against the stigma that surrounds people with mental illness.

Recovery is about testing one's mental health with life's challenges. One never knows what might happen today or tomorrow. Recovery is about finding out who you are and what you are, and accepting changes. Perhaps, a person was once a salesman at a particular point in time. However, when a person has a mental disorder like schizophrenia, they need to take another look at themselves and see that maybe being a salesman is no longer the right job for them, and is not who or what they are now. Recovery from mental illness is not just about changing jobs or occupations. It is about adapting again to the society in which one lives.

I think the most difficult thing a mentally ill person has to cope with is dealing with people who still have a lot of stigma, hatred, and discrimination towards the mentally ill. But today's world is changing. Recovery is about fighting for changes in the mental health system. People are being educated about mental illness by those who suffer from it, or by people who have families in which a mental illness exists.

You could share your own story of how you recovered from mental illness or know of someone that did, by talking to your senator or congressperson about the needs for the mentally ill, or by leading a support group in your church or synagogue.

Recovery from mental illness is a process throughout one's whole life. If someone is sick and needs their tonsils taken out, all they need to do to recover is to undergo an operation and eat lots of ice cream. Because mental illness lasts a lifetime, recovery is not that simple.

There are some people who cannot survive and feel recovery is not possible because the world does not accept them. This is why some commit suicide. It takes ability, strength, and faith in oneself to understand what type of recovery is possible.

I am not saying that a person with mental illness should choose the choices I made, the lifestyle I have, and the challenges that I have overcome as a mentally ill person, but one can certainly learn from what I have written. I feel that my story is a great example of recovery, considering the fact that I am an orthodox Jewish woman, and am someone that had to deal with Jewish people who are biased in the area of mental illness because of their lack of knowledge concerning this disease.

If you have a mental illness, I will now urge you to think about the circumstances in your life and how to cope with and recover from it. Therefore if I had to choose a definition for recovery, it would be **"LIVING LIFE"**.

CPSIA information can be obtained at www.ICGtesting.com
Printed in the USA
BVOW11s0036200815

414174BV00006B/46/P